RULES, DECISIONS, AND INEQUALITY

*This collection is dedicated
to the memory of*

Einneacháin Ó Flannagáin

and of

Kay and Grahame Ogden

Rules, Decisions, and Inequality

In Egalitarian Societies

Edited by
JAMES G. FLANAGAN
Department of Sociology and Anthropology
University of Southern Mississippi
and
STEVE RAYNER
Energy Division
Oak Ridge National Laboratory

HM
146
.R85
1988
West

ASU WEST LIBRARY

Avebury

Aldershot · Brookfield USA · Hong Kong · Singapore · Sydney

© J. G. Flanagan and S. Rayner, 1988

All rights reserved. No part of this publication may be reproduced, stored in a retrieval system, or transmitted in any form or by any means, electronic, mechanical, photocopying, recording, or otherwise without the prior permission of Gower Publishing Company Limited.

Published by

Avebury

Gower Publishing Company Limited,
Gower House, Croft Road, Aldershot,
Hants. GU11 3HR, England

Gower Publishing Company,
Old Post Road, Brookfield, Vermont 05036
USA

British Library Cataloguing in Publication Data
Rules, decisions and inequality in
   egalitarian societies.
   1. Social inequality
   I. Flanagan, James G., 1949- II. Rayner,
   Steve
   305

ISBN 0-566-05762-X

Printed by Kingprint International
Richmond, Surrey

Contents

Acknowledgements

This collection started life as a series of papers presented at the 84th Annual Meeting of the American Anthropological Association in Washington, D.C. Sally Falk Moore was discussant on that occasion, and the presenters all benefited from her insights. Following the AAA session, the editors sought additional papers to complete the symposium geographically and conceptually. We are grateful both to the original participants and to those who responded to our subsequent solicitation.

We also thank Patricia Lund who devoted considerable time and energy to careful copy editing, typesetting, and indexing of the manuscript. Without her help, this project may never have reached completion.

Contributors

James G. Flanagan is assistant professor of sociology and anthropology at the University of Southern Mississippi. Educated at the National University of Ireland, University College Cork (MA sociology), and at the University of Pennsylvania (PhD anthropology), he has conducted research in Ireland on bilingualism and in the Highlands of Papua New Guinea on kinship and politics among the Wovan people. His primary research interests are in social organization, the anthropology of law, and political anthropology. He is currently working on a book on the politics of endogamous marriage among the Wovan.

Steve Rayner's principal research interest is in the different concepts of fairness that institutional and organizational cultures use in decision making, especially in science and technology policy. He received his first degree in philosophy and theology from the University of Kent at Canterbury and a PhD in anthropology from University College London. He has studied grassroots political movements in the UK and the US for over twelve years. His current research addresses problems of global risk management. He is co-author (with Jonathan Gross) of *Measuring Culture*. Presently on the research staff of Oak Ridge National Laboratory, he has been a visiting scholar at Columbia University and Boston University School of Public Health. He was previously a research associate at the Russell Sage Foundation and the Centre for Occupational Community Research in the UK.

Davydd Greenwood received his doctorate in anthropology from the University of Pittsburgh. He became assistant professor of anthropology at Cornell University in 1970, has served as Chair of the Biology and Society major there, and is currently John S. Knight Professor of International Studies and Director of Cornell's Center for International Studies. He has held a number of research grants and fellowships, and served as principal investigator for several grant and funding programs. He has published numerous articles and three books, including *Unrewarding Wealth: Commercialization and the Collapse of Agriculture in a Spanish Basque Town; Nature, Culture, and Human History: A Bio-cultural Introduction to Anthropology;* and *The Taming of Evolution: The Persistence of Nonevolutionary Views in the Study of Humans.*

Stuart Henry received his doctorate in sociology from the University of Kent at Canterbury in 1976. He is currently associate professor of sociology at Eastern Michigan University, where he teaches criminological theory and white-collar crime. He has taught at polytechnics and universities in England and the United States and has written numerous articles for journals and magazines. His books include *Self-Help and Health*, which he coauthored with D. Robinson; *The Hidden Economy; Informal Institutions*, which he edited; and *Private Justice: Towards Integrated Theorising in the Sociology of Law.*

Gerald Mars, an anthropologist with an interest in modern societies, took his BA in economics and anthropology at Cambridge University and his PhD at the London School of Economics. He has held research and teaching positions at Oxford, Cambridge, and Newfoundland Universities and at Middlesex Polytechnic. Previously Reader and Head of the Centre for Health, Occupational and Community Research at North East London Polytechnic, he is currently Professor of Applied Anthropology in the Department of Management at

Cranfield Institute of Technology, England. He has published several books and over 40 academic papers.

Luther P. Gerlach received his doctorate from the University of London in 1960, and currently is professor of anthropology and adjunct professor of public affairs at the University of Minnesota. He has held visiting professorships, research fellowships, and consultantships at various institutions in the United States and Europe. He has published many articles in professional and popular journals, as well as two books, *People, Power, Change: Movements of Social Transformation* and *Lifeway Leap, the Dynamics of Change in America*, both of which were co-authored with Virginia Hine.

Ursula M. Gerlach was originally trained in nursing, but has assisted her husband in all his research. In their continuing studies in Kenya, she has been instrumental in gathering information from Digo women and children and has worked with Luther to produce their many documentary films and videos, including *Grassroots Energy* and *Energy, Resource Use and Systems Change*.

William Donner received his PhD from the University of Pennsylvania, Philadelphia, in 1985. The recipient of numerous grants and honors, including a postdoctoral fellowship at the University of Pennsylvania, he returned to the Solomon Islands in spring of 1987 to further his research on the traditional language of Sikaiana, its cultural preservation and change. Included in his publications is a lexicon of the Sikaiana language.

1 Introduction

JAMES G. FLANAGAN AND STEVE RAYNER

'If the broad problem in political anthropology is to understand the origin and variety of inequality, that in legal anthropology is to understand the maintenance of inequality.' Thus, Andrew Arno (1985:40) recently opened a broad review of legal anthropology. Indeed, Arno's formulation of the problem of explaining inequality need not be confined to the concerns of anthropology. Philosophy and the social sciences have shared an historic concern with the origin and maintenance of inequality. The study of other cultures has been invoked frequently to justify the enlightenment assumption that individual equality is the natural state of human organization from which inequality develops through the accumulation of restrictive and discriminatory rules. This position has had some unanticipated consequences for the study of human social organization.

The acceptance of a general evolutionary model that sees complex sociocultural forms as emerging from more simple egalitarian ones has led to the neglect of egalitarianism in anthropology. Egalitarianism remains a residual category, a sort of stasis to which societies would revert, through some sort of sociocultural inertia, if the wheels of culture were not relentlessly driven by necessary evolutionary differentiation.

Despite its infrequency in the ethnographic record, this conception of egalitarianism is maintained by the uncritical coexistence of a plethora of definitions that classify together radically different sociocultural organizations and structures as egalitarian.

Leacock and Lee (1982:159ff), reviewing the approaches of anthropologists to the study of gatherer-hunters, comment on the variety of definitions of egalitarianism that have been employed. These definitions range from a focus on reciprocity and generalized sharing to the direct acquisition or appropriation of natural resources by the community. Sometimes, the concept seems to be so broadly applied as to include all forms of social organization prior to the formation of the state. For example, in reasserting the historical primacy of egalitarianism, Michael Taylor (1982:3) writes:

> Egalitarian anarchic communities did in fact survive for millennia. Homo sapiens lived in such communities for nearly all of his forty or fifty thousand years. But eventually - in most cases in the last few centuries - they all but disappeared: absorbed, undermined, or destroyed by states.

It is undoubtedly true, in absolute terms, that the relative disparities in material condition are generally narrower in acephalous societies, chiefdoms, and big-man systems than those that exist within large states. However, it is questionable whether this contrast justifies the description of all stateless societies and, incidentally, the internal order of peasant communities, as egalitarian.

This book reverses the traditional evolutionary assumption to explore the origin and maintenance of equality in diverse organizational forms. Presenting case studies from Melanesia, Polynesia, Africa, the Middle East, Europe, and the United States, the essays gathered here critically examine the range of forms that have been glossed as egalitarian. Rather than counterposing community, smallness, and simplicity of egalitarian organization with the complexity of large market or bureaucratic systems, the authors demonstrate that egalitarian relationships are not simply non-hierarchical, but are achieved and maintained by the social and symbolic manipulation of often complex rules systems governing decision making. Hence, egalitarian systems of social organization place costly demands upon their members for participation and vigilance. Unless careful attention is paid to the preservation and enforcement of decision-making rules, egalitarian societies are likely to revert to hierarchical stratification (Rayner 1986). The instability of egalitarian decision making accounts for the schismatic tendencies of sects, cults, and communes described in the anthropological literature.

Although written by anthropologists, the papers assembled in this volume were selected to speak also to philosophers, sociologists, and political scientists, all of whom confront the same issues concerning the context and meaning of equality that arise out of a shared enlightenment heritage.

Egalitarianism in the state of Grace and the state of nature

Early discussions of the origins of inequality generally turned on the distinction between the nature of pre-social man and human society. Plato held that political inequality reflected natural differences in the innate faculties of men that suited them for different roles in the polity. However, this view was inverted in subsequent western thought, especially in Christian doctrine. Despite the highly stratified character of feudal society, particularly in the earthly hierarchy of its religious institutions, individual citizens of Christendom were deemed equal before God. Inequalities among individuals were introduced through the fall of Adam from the natural paradise of Eden and the introduction of sin to human relations. Hence, inequality was to be endured in this life for the protection of civil order in a sinful world and, thus, as a necessary constraint upon evil. By way of contrast, the mediaeval Christian expected no social inequality in the life hereafter.

Death was recognized as the great leveler long before the advent of Christianity. Horace wrote in the first century BC: 'Pale Death kicks his way equally into the cottages of the poor and the castles of kings.' However, those mediaeval Christians who would not wait for the next life attempted to hurry the onset of the biblical millennium promised in Revelation XX by emulating the egalitarian state of original Grace within sectarian communities such as those of the sixteenth-century Anabaptists in Germany (Cohn 1957) or the English Diggers of the seventeenth century (Hill 1975). If they eschewed sin in pursuit of the state of Grace, it was believed that men would live as brothers without inequalities of wealth and power.

3

The age of reason gave birth to a secular justification for the belief that egalitarianism was the original state of man by substituting the state of nature for the original state of Grace that preceded mankind's expulsion from Eden. Seventeenth-century English political philosopher Thomas Hobbes wrote in *The Leviathan*:

> Nature hath made men so equall, in the faculties of body, and mind; as that though there bee found one man sometimes manifestly stronger in body, or of quicker mind than another; yet when all is reckoned together, the difference between man, and man, is not so considerable, as that one man can thereupon claim to himselfe any benefit, to which another may not pretend, as well as he (Hobbes 1651:183).

The Hobbesian state of nature, for all its aggression, war, and possibility of imminent death at the hands of a fellow human (though not a fellow citizen), has long held a fascination for cultural evolutionary theorists. Nowhere outside the myths of the American West, a world populated by individuated gunslingers, each one merely a step ahead of the fractionally faster gun, has the ideal of male competition and male equality been so well described. The state of nature is a state of competitive equality. This equality, however, is the product of men's inability to subjugate others permanently. For Hobbes, in the last analysis, mankind's overall inclination is towards a 'perpetuall and restlesse desire of Power after power, that ceaseth onely in Death' (1651:161).

This viewpoint was developed in Rousseau's myth of the noble savage. Unburdened by the cares and inequities of the hierarchical state system, Rousseau's savage was free to engage in the noble pursuits of the complete person. Freedom, for Rousseau, was possible only in a community of equals. Entering into the social contract, however, inevitably robbed man of this natural equality. Differential rules, differentially applied, created an appearance of inequality. Although the evils of unfreedom were socially created, Rousseau was invariably pessimistic about society's ability to correct the tendency to social stratification.

Whereas, for Hobbes, inequality was a necessary component of the maintenance of good order, for Rousseau, inequality was an unnecessary and undesirable outcome of sociality itself. In this sense, Rousseau remained a creature of his Christian

4

heritage. His successors, the early socialists Fourier, Proudhon, Saint-Simon, and Owen, were crucial in entertaining the hope of restoring mankind to what they believed to be its pristine state of equality within society.

The evolutionary view of social inequality

Despite Marx's rejection of much of the early utopian socialist thinking, their idealized view of man's original state fitted perfectly into his dialectical theory of social transformation with its roots in Hegel's elaborate analysis of the master-slave relationship. Marx and Engels' view of the primitive community was dominated by their idea of the egalitarian relationships that obtained there. Drawing on Lewis Henry Morgan's (1877) description of Iroquois matrilineal descent-group organization, Engels wrote (1884, 1972:159) 'there cannot be any poor or needy - the communal household and the gens know their responsibilities toward the old, the sick and those disabled in war. All are equal and free - the women included.' Thus, even the elementary forms of interpersonal hierarchy arose, not with the sexual division of labor (that Engels acknowledges existed in the matrilineal gens), but with the reorganization of society from one based on kinship to one based on locality.

Like Rousseau, Marx, writing in 1858, saw ancient man as more consciously concerned with the complete person than his modern capitalist counterpart:

> Hence in one way the childlike world of the ancients appears to be superior; and this is so, in so far as we seek for closed shape, form and established limitation. The ancients provide a narrow satisfaction, whereas the modern world leaves us unsatisfied, or, where it appears to be satisfied with itself, is vulgar and mean (Marx 1964:82-83).

An important distinction is evident between the Marxian view of primitive equality and that of Hobbes and Rousseau. Marx and Engels' primitive equality was lodged firmly within a social organizational structure. The group is already organized as a social entity, structured along lines of kinship and descent and engaging in acts of war against other such groups. For both Rousseau and Hobbes, such equality existed only in the hypothetical pre-social state.

The publication of Charles Darwin's *The Origin of Species* (1859) radically affected the development of subsequent social theory. The traditional locus of debate about equality began to shift from the straightforward distinction between man and nature to the more elaborate interaction between genetic and environmental influences. The problematic relationship between the biological development and social development of humanity has remained one of the most disputed issues in scientific theory ever since.

Under the influence of Darwinism, the latter part of the nineteenth century witnessed a fundamental shift in the view of human nature away from the idealized egalitarian assumptions of seventeenth-century writers. The degenerationist arguments of Rousseau and his nineteenth-century counterparts were opposed by the new scientific progressivism. The new position carried powerful reverberations of Hobbes' doctrine concerning life in the state of nature as 'nasty, brutish and short.' The position is well stated by Sir John Lubbock:

> The true savage is neither free nor noble; he is a slave to his own wants, his own passions; imperfectly protected from the weather, he suffers from the cold by night and the heat of the sun by day; ignorant of agriculture, living by the chase, and improvident in success, hunger always stares him in the face, and often drives him to the dreadful alternative of cannibalism or death (1865).

According to the progressivists, prehistoric ancestors and 'primitive contemporaries' (Murdock 1934) alike lived not in some idealized egalitarian social order, but rather, subsisted merely a step ahead of the most radical of all dietary alternatives. Destitution was second only to death as a leveler of men. In this view, primitive equality was not a moral state but merely a practical lack of order and the social differentiation necessary for civil society.

Reviewing the development of the complex and interrelated terms 'culture' and 'civilization,' Stocking (1987) argues that both concepts took on hierarchical connotations during the nineteenth century. Under the influence of 'the inegalitarian assumptions of the emerging racialist physical anthropology' (1987:27), social thought gradually shifted its view of human interdependence from a position of egalitarian organicism to hierarchical progressivism. Discussions of egalitarianism and inequality shifted their focus from interpersonal relationships and the development of structural hierarchy within society to the ordering of societies along an evolutionary scale from savagery to civilization. Thus, the racialist progressivism of the nineteenth century does not directly address the issue of interpersonal equality that is our focus here. However, the perspective of a world consisting of 'an ordered hierarchy of social groups morally integrated by religion' (Stocking 1987: 27) provided a model within which all human relations could be conceived.

Darwinian biological evolutionism, that was to have such an impact on the development of western social theory, was presaged, albeit in programmatic form, in the social evolutionism of Auguste Comte. In his *Cours de Philosophie Positive* (1830-1842), Comte had outlined his 'great fundamental law' that human knowledge had passed through three theoretical states: theological, abstract, and scientific. The achievement of this new, scientific, positive level of human theorizing would unlock the key to understanding human society and human progress. Comtean progressivism provided the positivist underpinnings for the whole later development of evolutionary anthropology. What originated as the cultural product of a specific theoretical tradition became naturalized and was perceived as fundamental to human thought and human psychology. Thus, Langness (1980:13), commenting on the false attribution of such evolutionary theorizing to Lewis Henry Morgan, goes so far as to suggest that 'a hierarchical view of this sort is virtually fundamental to human thought.'

Whether perceived as the beneficial result of controlled competition (as in the utopia of Spencer, 1884) or as the degeneration of the social order (as in Engels), the emergence of inequality from primaeval egalitarianism is one of the central foci of nineteenth and early twentieth century evolutionary theorizing.

At the broad societal level, Tonnies (1887) described the general tendency of societies to shift from *gemeinschaft* to *gesellschaft*. Durkheim (1893) traced the evolution of society from *mechanical solidarity*, where members identify with each other because they are essentially the same, to *organic solidarity* where members identify with each other because of their reliance on each other to perform different but interrelated social tasks. At a more micro level, Michels and Weber addressed the evolution of complex inequality as an empirical process in voluntary organizations. Michels (1915), described the process by which democratically elected holders of supposedly rotating offices are able to win reelection due to advantages of incumbency. Reelection in turn leads to a *customary right to office*, and egalitarian democracy gives way to entrenched hierarchy. A similar process to Michels' famous *iron law of oligarchy* in political parties was described by Weber (1921) for religious sects as *routinization*; the process by which charismatic leadership of essentially egalitarian groups is replaced by the establishment of a bureaucratic hierarchy. Hence, in both the long and short terms, the evolutionary history of mankind has been characterized as a process of ever increasing differentiation of function, accompanied by social stratification. The human animal never works to achieve equality, but continues, in Hobbesean fashion, to lust after power.

Egalitarianism and evolution in political anthropology

The publication of *African Political Systems* (Fortes and Evans-Pritchard 1940) is viewed by most anthropologists as the beginning of modern political anthropology. In their introduction to that work, Fortes and Evans-Pritchard set up a model of three types of political organization found in Africa. One type 'consists of those societies which have centralized authority, administrative machinery, and judicial institutions' (1940:5). In these societies 'cleavages of wealth, privilege, and status correspond to the distribution of power and authority' (1940:5). Another type of social organization 'consists of those societies which lack centralized authority' and in which there are 'no sharp divisions of rank, status, and wealth' (1940:5). The first of these groups corresponds to state-level societies, the second consists of stateless societies. Inequality, in the form of hereditary chiefship or kingship, frequently is institutionalized in the former group but absent in the latter. Political roles in these state societies are 'hierarchically arranged in a series of superordinate and subordinate statuses' (Middleton and Tait 1958:2). In the stateless societies described in *African Political Systems*, social order is maintained by the balanced opposition of groups or segments of groups defined by unilineal descent principles.

The third type of social organization acknowledged by Fortes and Evans-Pritchard consists of small-scale hunters and gatherers among whom 'even the largest political unit embraces a group of people all of whom are united to one

8

another by ties of kinship' (1940:6).   Unfortunately, the ethnography included in *African Political Systems* is confined only to the first two types, perhaps due to the authors' uncertainty about the meaning and validity of discussing hunter-gatherer politics.   However, their object in devising the threefold typology was to provide an initial classification and to arrange these societies on a scale of increasing complexity, from those based on kinship through those based on lineage and descent to state-organized societies.

Refining the work of Fortes and Evans-Pritchard, Middleton and Tait (1958) drew attention to the complexities of those middle-range, uncentralized societies.   Some, particularly in Central Africa, lack corporate descent groups, and political authority is vested in chiefs and headmen (1958:3).   In others it is vested in age sets or age groups, and in still others political authority is vested in village councils (1958:3).   The papers assembled by Middleton and Tait are concerned only with those stateless societies in which political relations are articulated through the idiom of descent.   Such systems characteristically are composed of a series of hierarchically nested units in a 'state of continual segmentation and complementary opposition' (1958:7).   The structural units (whether defined purely in terms of descent i.e. minimal, medial, and maximal lineages, or in territorial terms i.e. hamlets, villages, tribes etc.) are 'regarded as complementary and formally equal, even if in actuality they are not so in population, wealth or in other ways' (1958:7).   Lacking the institutionalized mechanisms of social control that were familiar to western anthropologists, stateless societies became objects of intensive investigation and provided anthropology with its first intensively described cases of egalitarian societies.

The concept of equality employed here is worthy of some scrutiny.   The analytical unit is obviously the lineage or lineage segment.   Having arisen in the same structural process of segmentation, these units are equal by definition, irrespective of the power differentials that may exist between actual units.   Focusing on individuals in such systems, Fried (1967) differentiates egalitarian and hierarchical systems on the basis of the availability of status positions.   In egalitarian societies, according to Fried, there are as many status positions available as there are individuals to fill them.   The acceptance of age grading, the hierarchical ordering of males into a ranked series based on age, as compatible with a definition of an

9

egalitarian system (cf Schneider 1979) is consistent with this definition. The individual amasses power and wealth as he passes through the system but all individuals have an equal opportunity to pass through the system in their lifetime.

The value of both Fortes and Evans-Pritchard's and Middleton and Tait's volumes rests in their attempts to provide initial classifications of the variety of political systems in Africa. However, the contributors to both volumes are focusing on intergroup relations and are not concerned with the nuances of interpersonal relations conceived either as egalitarian or hierarchical. Nor does either volume address political relations in the many hunter-gatherer societies that remained anthropology's epitome of egalitarianism.

The mid-twentieth century structural-functionalism of Fortes, Evans-Pritchard, Middleton, and Tait spared little time for evolutionary speculation. However, the reemergence of a concern with history and social process in anthropology during the 1960's, in turn, rekindled widespread interest in the evolution of the state among both Marxist and non-Marxist scholars. Some of the newer evolutionary theorizing is richer than that of the iron-law-of-oligarchy school that preceded it by 50 to 100 years. For example, Carneiro's 'general principle of cultural development,' that 'since Neolithic times there has been a decrease in the number of autonomous political units and an increase in their size' (1978:206), may be pretty self-evident. However, he attributes these changes to a principle of competitive exclusion manifest in warfare. The processes of fusion, as Carneiro suggests, frequently were subverted by fissioning tendencies (1978:211), but the overall trend remained intact. Carneiro ties his principle of exclusion to the formation and agglomeration of supra-communal entities, not to the development of hierarchies. However, the assumption of increasing complexity is alive and well as many of Carneiro's colleagues tie both processes together and perceive the development of hierarchy as a direct outcome of state formation.

Service, in reviewing the major theoretical approaches to state formation, makes such an approach explicit. He argues (Service 1978:24) that the 'survival of the fittest, in Spencer's terminology, must have been an important factor in political evolution.' Such fitness was dependent on the organizational benefits that devolved from bureaucratic organization. These benefits, in turn, assured the 'continued growth in power of the bureaucratic organization itself.' Stratification is, thus, 'so closely coterminous with the state as to be virtually synonymous with it' (1978:27). The systemic, linear evolutionary imperative requires state formation, and states are synonymous with hierarchy. Thus, hierarchical organizations are both explained and justified.

The concept of 'sociocultural levels of integration,' first introduced by Julian Steward (1955), is one of the most frequently used analytical tools in assessing the power changes that occurred with the evolution of state-level societies. In a recent overview of anthropological approaches to the study of power, Richard Adams (1977) discusses the development of hierarchy as a simple outcome of the availability of power. 'The presence of higher levels of integration means that an increased amount of power is available in comparison with related societies that have fewer levels. In analytical terms, there is more power in the system because there are more energy forms available to control' (1977:402). Here, we find the reemergence of the old anthropological assumption that egalitarian societies are egalitarian simply because they do not have the capacity (sufficient controllable resources) to develop hierarchy. Once a means of controlling such resources becomes available, hierarchy and inequality will inevitably follow.

Interpersonal equality in contemporary anthropology

The 1960's also saw anthropology re-examining its approach to the study of interpersonal relations. Influenced by Fredrik Barth (1966), a number of anthropologists began to focus attention on the interactional strategies employed by individuals in their normal everyday encounters. Using an economic metaphor, social interactions were viewed as transactions (Kapferer 1976) in which individuals exchanged goods or messages and in which the calculating individual was oriented toward maximizing his/her own goals. Anthropological studies of politics became largely oriented to the study of individuals' acquisition and manipulation of power in local contexts (Schwartz 1968).

Consistent with Arno's assessment of the principal concerns of political anthropology with which we opened this discussion, the generation and maintenance of social inequality remained the central concern. Nonetheless, the renewed focus on the level of the individual, rather than on institutional integration, led some anthropologists to pursue new questions concerning the relative status of males and females in egalitarian systems and the relative status conferred by age (Baxter and Almagor 1978).

The dominant focus in anthropological theorizing remains fixed on structural relations. This focus locates inequality firmly in the domain of institutions and excludes egalitarian relationships from the domain of structure. The most elegant statement of this point of view appears in the work of Victor Turner: 'Structure, or all that which holds people apart, defines their differences, and constrains their actions, is one pole in a charged field, for which the opposite pole is communitas, or anti-structure, the egalitarian "sentiment for humanity" of which David Hume speaks' (1974:274). Strictly, communitas refers only to those relationships existing during the liminal period of initiation. It is anti-structural in the sense of existing outside the domain of the social - a fleeting return to the state of Grace. Yet, when Turner goes on to state that communitas tends to 'ignore, reverse, cut across, or occur outside of structural relationships' (1974:274), he returns the concept to the domain of everyday life and the distinction fails between communitas and the 'camaraderie found in everyday life.'

For Turner, structure is 'that which holds people apart, defines their differences, and constrains their actions....' The differentiating aspect of structure, however, can only be one of its own poles. Structure must also be that which holds people together, provides a notion of identity, and permits acceptable interpretation of signs. In this sense, structure must be an organization of contradictions (Kelly 1977) or, as Edgerton (1985) has noted, must contain within it both 'exceptions' and rules about breaking rules.

'No matter what their ideology may have been, members of our species have never doubted that inequalities exist among human beings' (Adams 1977:395). Anthropologists have devoted considerable time to their efforts to explain the origin and maintenance of such inequalities. In doing so, however, they have banished equality to the fringes of anthropological concern, to the level of the non-problematic, the non-structural, or perhaps even anti-structural. The object of the papers in this collection is to retrieve this component of anti-structure and return it to its proper domain.

The present approach

In reversing the predominant assumption about social development - that complex hierarchies develop from an initial egalitarian state by the accretion of rules - our purpose is not to establish an ontological proposition about the original state of mankind. We may suspect from primate behavior that man's ancestors established pecking orders as the basis of sociality. We may intuit that egalitarianism was the subsequent development of already social beings to counteract biological inequalities of physical strength or practical cunning. In the final analysis, prehistory is ambivalent, and empirical evidence is ambiguous. In any case, we do not need a prehistoric charter to make a moral case for equality in today's world. Such a debate about the original state of mankind would be pointless.

The purpose of reversing the predominant evolutionary assumption is rather to discover what insights a change of vantage point can bring to the subtle and interesting interplay between hierarchy and equality in real societies. It is perhaps ironic that the very societies that have produced theories of the evolution of inequality are the same ones that, despite great concentrations of wealth, have been developing greater equality before the law, broader access to education, and more widely distributed public health benefits than they have achieved since the golden age of equality that supposedly preceded the development of the state.

These three benefits are representative of the three great equalities, all of which are dealt with by the authors collected here. They are moral equality, equality of opportunity, and equality of condition. In all three respects, modern industrial society represents an improvement over its immediate antecedents for Europeans, Asians, and the non-indigenous peoples of North America. Yet, the uneven distribution of economic wealth and the increasing sophistication of the industrial state has led commentators to concentrate on complexity and inequality, sometimes even conflating these qualities. We do not wish to deny the inequalities of wealth and power in the modern world, but to suggest that as the size of the economic gap between rich and poor may have grown, in other respects society has become more egalitarian.

This apparently paradoxical fact of the coexistence, even the interdependence, of equality and inequality is a central theme for a number of the contributors to this volume. Using cases from cooperatives in Spain, Britain, and Israel, as well as communities in Oceania and Africa, they clearly demonstrate that the coexistence of hierarchy and equality is not exclusive to the mainstream of industrial society. Greenwood, Donner, and Flanagan extensively discuss the simultaneous maintenance of inequality and equality within the same social system. Their contributions emphasize the importance of specifying role relationships and interactional settings when discussing egalitarianism.

The contributors to this volume all emphasize the importance of analysis at the behavioral rather than the merely ideological level. Rayner's concentration on the rules of decision making indicates, contrary to traditional assumptions of organizational simplicity, that maintaining egalitarian relationships may require complex rules systems. Such rules are designed to promote the mutual substitutability of elements (individual or collective) in the decision making system. However, although extensive in their complexity, these kinds of rules are deliberately constructed to provide as little differentiating information about individuals as possible.

Rayner's case studies establish two distinctive levels at which concerns about strict equality of condition are articulated. He uses the International Marxist Group to illustrate concerns about preserving collective solidarity by balancing the relative decision making power of different factions or segments in an organization. His example of the American direct-action environmentalist groups reflects concerns with interpersonal equality in decision making. The distinction between collective and individual egalitarianism is reflected one way or another throughout the collection.

Greenwood places his emphasis on the promotion of collective solidarity as the key concern of the Basque collectives that have been dubbed egalitarian by economists and political scientists alike. Clearly, the principle of mutual substitutability does not apply to the distinctive division of labor and the principles of proportional reward operated by the cooperators. Theirs is a system of equity rather than strict equality. Fairness, embodied in a combination of moral equality before the law and equality of opportunity, rather than identity or sameness, is the principle that is used to ensure the solidarity of these cooperative enterprises.

Henry deals with cooperatives that pursue ideals closer to strict-equality principles than to the equity system of the Basque country. Examining the interaction of egalitarian cooperatives within a wider cultural framework that is relatively hierarchical, Henry's account of the problems of community justice highlights the difficulties of operating simultaneously in two contexts. While ignoring free riders introduces inequalities in the coop, resorting to the enforcement mechanisms of market society to resolve free-rider problems reproduces the inegalitarian authority structures of the wider society. Henry's considerations emphasize the immense difficulties and investment in human resources that are involved in actually achieving and maintaining a strict-egalitarian state.

Mars also addresses the issue of maintaining strict equality in a cooperative setting. He describes the emergence of an elite and a proletariat in the kibbutz, in violation of formal rules that were designed to maintain the mutual substitutability of elements through job rotation. However, unlike his distinguished predecessors, such as Weber and Michels, Mars does not attribute the change to the gradual accretion of restrictive hierarchical rules, but to control over the group boundary. It is also of interest to note that inequality is concealed, not by a free-floating ideology of equality that has somehow survived since the kibbutz was founded, but by placing the emergent proletariat outside of the group boundary and appointing the elite as guardians of that boundary.

Theoretical concentration on the development of complexity and inequality from simple egalitarian societies or organizations has encouraged neglect of the obverse case. There is very little theorizing about how equality develops out of hierarchy. The Gerlachs' case study provides some perspective on this development among the Digo of Kenya. The Gerlachs show how the elaboration of rules systems, rather than their elimination, may accompany the development of equality.

Of particular interest is the simultaneous manipulation of interpersonal and intergroup relationships used by the Digo to dismantle the historical basis for inequality among them. The resolution of a dispute about the burial site for a deceased relative asserts the collective equality of previously master and slave lineages. Entrepreneurial activity gives a young man the opportunity to redefine previously hierarchical relationships to his mother's brother. For the Digo, egalitarianism is the product of the tension between collectivism and individualism in their culture and history.

Donner's article on interpersonal relationships in Polynesia touches on many of the themes raised elsewhere in the book.

He emphasizes the simultaneous cohabitation of equality and inequality in the same system and, thus, the need to specify role relationships and interactional settings when discussing egalitarianism. Moral equality is maintained on Sikaiana through religious affirmation of equality before God. Equality of condition is manifested through role interchangeability and exerted through constraints on conspicuous consumption and behavior. Group solidarity is asserted through toddy drinking.

In the context of the other contributions to this volume, Donner's argument makes it hard to resist speculation that societies practicing collective egalitarianism will favor strict equality of condition, while equality of opportunity is preferred by individualistic egalitarians. However, further inquiry with a statistically valid sample of egalitarian social groups would be necessary to justify such a generalization.

The final article takes us geographically furthest from our starting point in this book. Conceptually it completes a circle. Concentrating on the individual, rather than the collective dimension of equality, Flanagan focuses on the rules that promote interpersonal equality in the face of institutionalized hierarchy and biological inequalities.

Resonating the Gerlachs' theme of interdependence, Flanagan does not merely argue that hierarchy and equality coexist, but that the creation of strict-equality relationships in an otherwise hierarchical setting must be conceived as an integral part of the social structure, rather than as a domain of ritual or playful anti-structure.

Such a perspective finally dissolves the dichotomy between equality and hierarchy, except as a convenient ideal-typical shorthand. Instead, we can recognize the need to examine the structure of actual human relationships as potentially measurable elements in rules systems. Since rules systems are systems of information, the mapping of rules in this way offers anthropology the opportunity to make systematic comparisons of social units and of individual roles within social units, based on what people do rather than on *ad hoc* judgments about the norms that they reproduce in speech.

Bibliography

Adams, Richard 1977. 'Power in Human Societies.' In *The Anthropology of Power* (eds) Raymond Fogelson and Richard Adams. New York: Academic Press.

Arno, Andrew 1985. 'Structural Communication and Control Communication: An Interactionist Perspective on Legal and Customary Procedures for Conflict Management.' In *American Anthropologist* 87:40-55.

Barth, Fredrik 1966. 'Models of Social Organization.' Occasional Paper 23. London: Royal Anthropological Institute.

Baxter, P.T.W. and Uri Almagor (eds) 1978. *Age, Generation and Time.* New York: St. Martin's Press.

Carneiro, Robert L. 1978. 'Political Expansion as an Expression of the Principle of Competitive Exclusion.' In *Origins of the State* (eds) Ronald Cohen and Elman Service. Philadelphia: ISHI.

Cohn, N. 1957. *The Pursuit of the Millennium.* London: Secker & Warburg.

Comte, Auguste 1830-42. *Cours de Philosophie Positive.* Paris: Bachelier. (Translated and condensed by Harriet Martineau. London: Bell, 1896).

Darwin, Charles 1958 (orig. 1859). *The Origin of Species.* New York: New American Library.

Durkheim, Emile 1893. *De La Division du Travail Social.* Paris: Alcan. Translation 1933. *Division of Labor in Society.* New York: Free Press.

Edgerton, Robert B. 1985. *Rules, Exceptions and Social Order.* Los Angeles: University of California Press.

Engels, Frederick 1972 (orig. 1884). *The Origin of the Family, Private Property and the State.* New York: New World Paperbacks.

Fortes, M. and E. Evans-Pritchard (eds) 1940. *African Political Systems*. London: Oxford University Press.

Fried, Morton 1967. *The Evolution of Political Society*. New York: Random House.

Hill, C. 1975. *The World Turned Upside Down*. Harmondsworth: Penguin Books.

Hobbes, Thomas 1651. *Leviathan*. Reprinted 1968. Harmondsworth: Penguin Books.

Kapferer, B. 1976. *Transaction and Meaning*. Philadelphia: ISHI.

Kelly, Raymond 1977. *Etoro Social Structure*. Ann Arbor: Michigan University Press.

Langness, L.L. 1980. *The Study of Culture*. Novato, California: Chandler & Sharp.

Leacock, E. and R. Lee (eds) 1982. *Politics and History in Band Societies*. London: Cambridge University Press.

Lubbock, John 1865. *Pre-historic Times, As Illustrated by Ancient Remains, and the Manners and Customs of Modern Savages*. London.

Marx, K. 1964. *Pre-capitalist Economic Formations*. London: Lawrence & Wishart. Original 1857-58. *Formen die der Kapitalistischen Produktion vorhergehen (uber den Prozess der der Bildung des Kapitalverhaltnisses oder der Ursprunglichen Akkumulation vorhergeht)*.

Michels, Robert 1915. *Political Parties: A Sociological Study of the Oligarchical Tendencies of Modern Democracy*. New York: Hearst.

Middleton, J. and D. Tait (eds) 1958. *Tribes Without Rulers*. London: Routledge and Kegan Paul.

Morgan, L.H. 1877. *Ancient Society*. New York: Holt.

Murdock, George P. 1934. *Our Primitive Contemporaries.* New York: Macmillan.

Rayner, Steve 1986. 'The Politics of Schism: Routinization and Social Control in the International Socialists/Socialist Workers Party.' In *Power, Action and Belief* (ed) John Law. Sociological Review Monograph 32. London: Routledge and Kegan Paul.

Schneider, Harold 1979. *Livestock and Equality in East Africa.* Bloomington: Indiana University Press.

Schwartz, Marc (ed) 1968. *Local Level Politics.* Chicago: Aldine.

Service, Elman 1978. 'Classical and Modern Theories of the Origins of Government.' In *Origins of the State* (eds) Ronald Cohen and Elman R. Service. Philadelphia: ISHI.

Spencer, Herbert 1884. *The Man Versus the State.* London: Williams and Nongate.

Steward, Julian 1955. *Theory of Culture Change.* Champagne: University of Illinois Press.

Stocking, George 1987. *Victorian Anthropology.* New York: Macmillan.

Taylor, M. 1982. *Community, Anarchy and Liberty.* Cambridge: Cambridge University Press.

Tonnies, Ferdinand 1887. *Gemeinschaft und Gesellschaft.* Leipzig: Fues. Translation 1957. *Community and Society.* East Lansing: Michigan State University Press.

Turner, Victor 1974. *Dramas, Fields and Metaphors.* Ithaca: Cornell University Press.

Weber, Max 1921. *Wirtschaft und Gesellschaft I.* Tubingen: J.C.B. Mohr. Translation 1967. *The Theory of Social and Economic Organization.* New York: Macmillan.

2 The rules that keep us equal: complexity and costs of egalitarian organization

STEVE RAYNER

ABSTRACT

The growth of inequality in simple egalitarian organizations is often attributed to an increase in the number and complexity of behavioral rules. This paper presents a counter example in which a Trotskyist organization generated expansive rules for factions to preempt the emergence of oligarchy. The IMG is compared to the American Abalone and Clamshell Alliances that applied strict-equality rules to individuals to maintain egalitarian consensus. The paper concludes that it is not the number and complexity of rules that promote inequality, but their intricacy; a simple, but mathematically precise, concept that describes the extent to which elements in a rules system are mutually substitutable.

The pervasive assumption in social science is that hierarchical rules are needed to promote longevity of institutions because of the perceived instability of primitive democracy. This state of strict equality of condition is vividly summarized by Lenin's *What is to be Done?*, as the condition where everyone does everything and nothing gets done. Such organizations are prone to organizational schism due to three factors. (1) Members become frustrated with the inability of the group to coordinate its activities to achieve its declared aims. (2) The absence of hierarchical authority for arbitrating internal disputes over policies or organization leads to factionalism (Rayner 1979). (3) The inability of major contributors to the group's activities to control free riders leads them to withdraw their support (Olson 1965).

Specialization of roles may be assumed to improve the group's efficiency in pursuit of its explicit goals, provide arbitration methods for disputes, and permit the enforcement of sanctions against free riders. Thus, hierarchical rules have commanded the attention of scholars because they seem to have imposed order where previously anarchy prevailed. However, the impression that social inequality develops because hierarchical rules gradually replace egalitarian rulelessness is misleading. Egalitarian social organization depends on rules systems that, in fact, may be more expansive and complex than those required for hierarchical society.

For the purposes of the following discussion it is worth distinguishing at least three types of social rules; differentiating rules (hierarchical), homogenizing rules (strict-equality), and equal-opportunity rules (equity). Each of the last two types of rules are characteristic principles of different sorts of egalitarianism. Both sorts assume moral equality. That is to say, both endow all members with the same inherent personal worth. However, each of the two types of egalitarianism approach the practical questions of the accumulation of material wealth and political power in different ways.

Homogenizing rules are characteristic of social systems based on strict equality. The aim of such systems is to maintain equality of condition between all members. The accumulation of private property is inimical to such a system, so rules of communal ownership may be applied, as among the Hutterites (Bennett 1967). Alternatively, rules of poverty may be used to ensure homogeneity of endowments, as among Christian friars or in certain Buddhist monastic orders (Schumann 1973). In this case, it is clear that the subsistence level of ownership is the easiest to monitor in a socially undifferentiated form of organization lacking accountants and tax officers to police its membership.

Equal-opportunity rules represent a different sort of egalitarian vision; that in which everyone has the same initial rights to participate, but where the accumulation of goods or political influence by individuals is treated largely as a matter

21

of preference. Those who do not accumulate such endowments are seen to fail to do so because they prefer to avoid stress, to take more leisure time, or to study. Provided that unfair means are not employed, competition between putative equals is not prevented by equal-opportunity rules. Although uneven accumulation of personal property is permitted, perhaps even admired, inherited wealth is not. Equal-opportunity rules are invoked to restrict unfair advantages accruing to some individuals in succeeding generations. The contrast between these two types of egalitarianism may be summarized by the emphasis on strict equality in the first case and on equity in the second. Wildavsky (1984) uses the term equity to describe what I call strict equality. I prefer to apply equity to equality of opportunity, rather than to strict equality of condition, for etymological reasons and because of the absence of a convenient term for systems employing equality of opportunity.

The problem with real-life egalitarian social systems is that they tend to mix both equity rules and strict-equality rules in the same context. Often, the strict-equality model provides an ideological anchor for a system that actually operates closer to the equity principle. Of course, we also know that, even in the strictest-equality systems, some are more equal than others, and charismatic leaders may exert an entrepreneurial influence over the decisions of the whole group. However, voluntary groups, even under the influence of charismatic leaders or behind-the-scenes powerbrokers, often adopt explicit rules systems that correspond to the strict-equality model. These groups are especially prone to the problems of schism, for while a charismatic leader may resolve disputes in the short term, long-term rivals will accuse the leader of violating the group's egalitarian principles and split off (Rayner 1986), especially if exit costs are low (Hirschman 1970).

However, the choice between instability or routinized hierarchy is not inevitable. Indeed, there follow two cases where egalitarian organization was maintained as the basis of flourishing voluntary organizations. In each case, this was achieved, at high cost, by the operation of quite substantial rules systems. Although they look like straightforward equal-opportunity rules, they actually go much further in enforcing strict equality of condition, even in the face of some considerable division of labor. These are 'the rules that keep us equal.'

Faction rules in the International Marxist Group

The first example is drawn from my own fieldwork on the social organization of British Trotskyist and Maoist groups during the 1970's (Rayner 1979). My principal focus was on the relationship between the phenomenon of rapid schism that characterized such organizations (Rayner 1986) and their tendency toward utopian and millenarian expectations of the future (Rayner 1982). However, one group, out of a total of about forty, exhibited a pattern of stability and growth uncharacteristic of its peers. That was a national organization of some one thousand members called the International Marxist Group (IMG).

The IMG was proclaimed as the British section of the United Secretariat of the Fourth International in 1968, and received full recognition at the Ninth World Congress the following year. However, the emergence of the group had been preceded by a long period of preparation dating back to the great split in the Trotskyist Fourth International, which occurred in 1953. Supporters of one international faction, the International Committee of the Fourth International, already were well organized in Britain, and subsequently formed the core of one of the IMG's rivals, the Workers' Revolutionary Party (WRP). Supporters of the International Secretariat, later the United Secretariat, of the Fourth International were left scattered and disorganized by the split. It was a long task to regroup them effectively, but by 1969, the IMG was embarked on a path of steady growth in numbers and influence that would carry them through the following decade.

In particular, it should be noted that the IMG did not suffer from the crippling scale of schism, mass expulsion, and membership turnover that beset its chief rivals between 1968 and 1978. Admittedly, the group suffered three splits, in 1970, 1974, and 1975 respectively. However, the total numbers involved in all three were less than 45 people, compared to the hundreds that passed through the ranks of the Workers' Revolutionary Party (WRP) and the International Socialists/ Socialist Workers' Party (IS/SWP) during the same period (Rayner 1986).

There were three major organizational differences between the IMG and its principal rivals, The International Socialists/ Socialist Workers' Party and the Workers' Revolutionary Party. First, the IMG did not develop under the aegis of a single charismatic leader or tiny clique of close colleagues as did the IS/SWP and WRP. Second, the IMG did not develop the same level of hostility to competing groups as its rivals. It never declared itself to be the sole revolutionary nucleus in Britain. Third, the IMG developed an internal democracy that guaranteed the rights of factions to organize and, furthermore, ensured them access to the discussion and decision-making apparatus of the whole group.

The key factor here is the legitimation of factions. As I shall argue, institutionalized factionalism limits the ambitions of individuals and cliques, reduces strife and schism, and promotes stable egalitarian organization. In contrast, voluntary organizations that prohibit open factions tend to be oligarchical and unstable. Divergent views within the group are forced into covert organization that frequently leads to schism. This is largely because of the limited range of sanctions available to those seeking to control organizations with explicitly egalitarian ideologies (Douglas 1978).

Demotion in a hierarchy or restriction of access to the public goods provided by an egalitarian group are not practical sanctions, because hierarchies are not recognized, and restriction violates the egalitarian ethic. Expulsion is the only credible penalty. So, when disputes in voluntary organizations cannot be resolved by resort to precedent or hierarchy, one faction will be tempted to accuse another of being outsiders or traitors who have, therefore, forfeited their rights of equal participation in the group. The very fact of organizing covert factions in groups where factions are forbidden, such as the WRP, is grounds to justify this kind of expulsion (Rayner 1979).

Expulsion is a tool that is used frequently by ambitious members of voluntary organizations wishing to routinize the group under their own leadership (Rayner 1986). Forcing factions into the vulnerable status of an illegitimate opposition that can be expelled easily requires only one simple rule; there shall be no factions. This single rule has helped many a voluntary group along the bitter path from equality to hierarchy. On the other hand, maintaining the rights of factions to exist within a framework of equal competition between ideas requires more complex rules as well as guidelines for their interpretation. We shall see that such complex egalitarian rules systems impose costs on organizations that enforce them. But first, let us see how these rules for maintaining factional equality operated in the IMG.

Tendencies and factions

Although egalitarian, the IMG possessed a degree of compact hierarchy with branch committees and a central committee for coordinating national activity. However, in contrast with other British far-left organizations, the IMG maintained a high level of accessability to these committees for different viewpoints within the organization. There was never an entrenched leadership faction such as those that characterized the WRP and SWP. The IMG permitted opposition to the leadership or majority position to be organized freely, without constraints based on branch membership or geographical area. It did this by recognizing two sorts of structures, tendencies and factions.

Tendencies were organized groupings of individuals from various branches, who had differences with the majority of the IMG on a limited range of specific issues. They were constituted formally by 20 or so members declaring that they were establishing a tendency on particular issues, and notifying the Central Committee accordingly. The Central Committee had the prerogative of granting or refusing recognition to a tendency. However, it would have been a serious step to withhold recognition, as this might have provoked more extensive disagreement, possibly forcing the opposition into covert factionalism.

Tendencies could be declared at any time, but most usually in the three-month discussion period prior to a national conference. They were dissolved when the issue was deemed to be settled, usually by conference decision. However, a tendency could continue between conferences, in which case it was likely to expand its original platform and convert itself into a faction. Exceptions were permitted to the numerical requirements for recognition of a tendency if the issues that it raised were considered by the Central Committee to be sufficiently important. For example, at the April 1978 conference, tendency rights were granted to a group of only seven or eight, whilst the largest tendency had almost 400 supporters.

A faction was set up when a minority felt that its differences with the majority were so fundamental that to continue along the course set by the existing leaders would lead to the political degeneration of the organization. Once again, factions declared themselves to the Central Committee, that had the right to grant or withhold recognition. Usually the leadership recognized a faction even if it felt that the issues at stake only merited the recognition of tendency status. To refuse recognition could be regarded by dissidents as evidence of the Central Committee's degeneration that caused the faction to declare itself in the first place.

Unlike tendencies, factions were not required to declare a limited range of issues on which they dissented from the majority. On the contrary, factions were expected to develop a comprehensive critique of the majority policies. Often, organizational grievances were cited as evidence of the Central Committee's political failure. But this sometimes merely reflected the frustration of a disgruntled tendency whose document was not published on time by the central office.

Once recognized, members of factions and tendencies had the right to hold their own internal meetings, regardless of whether they were members of different branches or committees. This is specifically forbidden within the Workers' Revolutionary Party, the Socialist Workers' Party, the Communist Party, and most other democratic-centralist organizations of the British left. In these organizations, members of different branches are permitted only to meet and organize political activity opposed to the majority position at higher committees of the party. Furthermore, factions and tendencies in the IMG were entitled to equal space in internal bulletins to put forward their positions, regardless of their numerical strength.

Tendencies originally were known by names, such as the London Opposition, or The Tendency, but those that emerged after 1973 generally were identified by letters as Tendency A, B, C, etc., rather than by the names of leaders, descriptive terms, or geographical locations. This policy was introduced because it was felt that the adoption of certain names was provocative, and caused unnecessary tension in debate. For example, the use of the name Bolshevik Tendency upset other members of the IMG who felt that they were being implicitly accused of Menshevism.

Factions and tendencies did not seem to follow geographical lines, except when particularly strong cadres were able to win over a whole branch. This would seem to indicate good communications between the branches and with the center, and a free flow of information throughout the organization. This is in strong contrast with the covert factions that occasionally arise in other far-left groups. In these cases, factions tend to be regional because of restrictions on meeting outside of the official branch structure.

The formal structure of factions and tendencies in the IMG was flexible and varied depending on the nature and range of issues involved. Generally speaking, a faction would elect a steering committee, organize local committees, and hold regular meetings. A faction had the right to impose its own rules (i.e. rights of expulsion) on members so long as these did not lead members to contravene the public positions of the IMG as a whole. A faction, therefore, functioned as a microcosm of the larger group.

A tendency was organized much more loosely, perhaps with a national steering committee. Unlike a faction, a tendency did not have disciplinary rights over members because its platform was limited to the issues specified at its foundation. A tendency was not allowed to add issues to its platform, unless it applied for faction status. Tendency members often disagreed fundamentally with each other over issues not specified in the tendency's platform. Indeed, in principle, it was possible for an IMG member to belong to more than one tendency if their platforms were concerned with different aspects of the group's policy or strategy.

Tendencies and factions did not break away from the IMG, or find themselves expelled from it, as did most of the covert factions in the WRP or the unofficial tendencies and factions in the IS/SWP. This is, at least partly, because the formalization of factions obstructed the concentration of power in the hands of a few individuals and served to depersonalize political power struggles within the organization. The tolerance of open factions reduced the likelihood of significant schisms, expulsions, and cases of individual disaffection that would otherwise have led to a high rate of membership turnover. The consequent relative stability of membership meant that the leadership of the IMG was more accountable to its membership than was the case with the WRP or the IS/SWP. In these organizations, the higher turnover of the rank and file meant that membership tended to be less experienced and more ready to accept the positions of the established leadership.

The existence of recognized factions in the IMG, furthermore, facilitated effective challenges to its leadership, that consequently was more responsive than the unassailable regimes of Gerry Healy in the WRP and Tony Cliff in the IS/SWP. The fact that the IMG did not produce a single dominant leader of the order of Healy or Cliff undoubtedly was due, in part, to the structure of factions and tendencies acting to block the careers of individual leaders who appeared to be bent upon entrenching their authority over the organization as a whole, whilst facilitating the emergence of new leading figures.

The relative freedom of the IMG from large-scale schisms of the sort that beset its principal rivals can be accounted for, to a considerable extent, by the same structures. Where factions are legitimated by the leadership, and operate quite openly, they cannot be portrayed as sinister and secretive sects bent upon subverting the democratic decision-making processes of the organization.

The assignment of a neutral name to each tendency or faction, such as Tendency A, etc., reduced the extent to which its success or failure could be identified with the names of its leading figures. This served to depersonalize political disagreement to some extent, and also made it more difficult for opponents to vilify the faction as a personal clique. For a covert faction, such accusations often are true, since, being covert, it is set up through personal contacts and is likely to be concentrated in a particular geographical area under the leadership of a powerful personality. Furthermore, the covert faction tends to restrict the number of its public spokespersons in order not to expose all of its supporters to disciplinary action. Therefore, fewer members have the opportunity to achieve acknowledgement as intermediate leaders.

The formal recognition of opposition in the IMG, embodied in structural mechanisms allowing for the formation of factions and tendencies, brought it stability combined with steady growth. However, the cost of this strategy was high. The rule allowing equal space to all tendencies in its internal publications meant that the group as a whole was forced to invest valuable resources, time, and money, circulating the viewpoint of what may have been a very small part of its membership. The cost of the 1978 conference came to L8,000 for an organization of less than 1,000 people.

As the IMG grew, the difficulty of maintaining adequate communication between all the members of the organization became increasingly challenging. In general, toleration of factions in a voluntary organization seems to depend upon a high level of understanding of a variety of viewpoints. The whole system of tendencies and factions and the constraints on the emergence of individual leaders in the IMG depended upon the maintenance of an efficient communication network and frequent face-to-face contact of the membership. Such a system, however, places its own strains on an organization, since the obligation upon the leadership to be seen to be dealing evenhandedly with minority tendencies might prove frustrating to the majority who feel that their program is being held back in order to avoid causing a major rift with the minority.

Despite these problems, the rules requiring even-handed treatment of all factions, irrespective of size and influence, worked well for the IMG at a time when other groups of the revolutionary left were beset by crises. The IS/SWP expanded its membership from two to three thousand during the 1970's, but it underwent a series of damaging splits and recessions and suffered from a very high turnover of members (Rayner 1986). The Workers' Revolutionary Party during the same period split and contracted.

At the end of the April 1978 conference of the IMG, all of the tendencies voluntarily disbanded, and the organization as a whole appeared to have achieved a remarkable degree of unanimity and a clear sense of political and organizational direction. However, by this point, the IMG had encountered a setback in its pattern of growth, that seems to have stemmed from strains encountered by individuals giving a high level of commitment to the organization over an extended period. The IMG had maintained a steady growth rate from 400 in 1974, to just under 1,000 in 1978. This was achieved with a turnover that reliable sources described as minuscule. However, in 1978, this pattern changed. The IMG recruited between 150-200 members, but lost about the same number, including some veterans who had been active in the organization for many years. Whilst not renouncing their support for the IMG, or even disengaging from active politics, a number of individuals dropped out of membership. This problem was not a total surprise in an organization that maintained a high level of activity with an exceptionally low turnover of members.

Unlike the refugees from the IS/SWP and the WRP, these ex-members of the IMG did not form tiny sects of their own or drift out of revolutionary politics altogether. They remained active and often in close contact with each other and with the IMG. It would appear that this lapsing of membership had more to do with the long-term strain of the level of commitment that the IMG required from its members than it had to do with political disaffection. This sort of loss from exhaustion must be counted as one of the costs of maintaining a system of factions that requires a high level of group activity and debate if it is not going to lapse into the sort of faction warfare stimulated by leadership oligarchy that occurred in the WRP and IS/SWP.

As my fieldwork was completed in 1979, I do not know if this organizational stress was a factor in the subsequent decision of the IMG to disband formally and enter the Labour Party. However, since the practice of *entryism*, the infiltration of a Trotskyist group into a social-democratic party, is an established mode of operation for these kinds of organization, and because of the previous structural stability of the IMG, I am inclined to believe that the decision was based on political rather than organizational considerations.

The egalitarian rules governing factions in the IMG look very much like equity rules. They were designed to ensure equality of opportunity for all viewpoints, to protect minorities from expulsion, as well as to guarantee such factions equal space in documents and equal time at conferences to express differences with the majority, regardless of size and composition. The first thing to notice about these rules is that they are quite detailed and expansive. On the other hand, only one rule would have been necessary to create hierarchy, the rule that was, in fact, instituted by the charismatic leaders of the WRP and the IS/SWP in consolidating their own oligarchical hierarchies. This rule can be summed up in two words, 'No factions!,' thus, providing the opportunity for the prospective hierarchists to expel opponents and consolidate bureaucratic control over the group as a whole.

A second point is also worthy of notice. We have already noted that, in principle, equity rules are quite compatible with an uneven distribution of endowments. These are rules about process, the way the game is played, rather than about outcomes. However, closer examination of the rules of fair play in the IMG reveals a strong element of strict equality that suggests that the distinction between equity and strict equality may not be possible in practice. In effect, the rules are designed to make the resources available to each faction mutually substitutable for those of any other, so that each can engage in the battle of ideas on the same footing. In effect, the IMG provides an empirical illustration of the argument, advanced theoretically in mathematical economics (Schulze 1980), that equity rules, designed to promote fair

30

competition, may have to amount to strict-equality rules in practice. A game can never be fair (in the sense of equal rather than reasonable) when the resources for play are divided unevenly. Imagine persuading friends to play Monopoly with an unequal initial distribution of toy money! Genuine attempts to achieve equality of access to decision making must, it seems, reduce to strict equality so that all players have access to the same resources.

But, the rules system operated by the IMG was palpably unfair in one important respect. It imposed an inequity on the numerical majority, or members of large factions, who received fewer resources per capita than did smaller factions. Egalitarian rules, enforced at the collective level of equal treatment for all factions, may generate unfair (i.e. unequal) distribution of resources at the individual level. This was recognized by the membership, but tolerated in the interests of internal peace and organizational stability.

The second case study I wish to examine in this paper, therefore, is one in which egalitarian rules of decision making are applied at the individual level. The example is provided by the decision-making procedures adopted by both the Clamshell and Abalone Alliances that emerged into the public eye during the attempted occupations of the Seabrook (New Hampshire) and Diablo Canyon (California) nuclear power plant sites during the late 1970's and early 1980's.

Individual equality in decision making: The Clamshell and Abalone Alliances

The Clams and Abalones are both alliances of local direct-action groups dedicated to eliminating nuclear generating technology at both local and global levels. Each alliance was formed to obstruct the construction and operation of nuclear power plants by any combination of non-violent activity that was available to them. However, these alliances are quite different from local NIMBYs (O'Hare 1977), the not-in-my-backyard intervenor groups, whose tactics usually have been confined to supporting prominent individuals in legal or regulatory obstruction of specific plants. Direct-action alliances, on the ·other hand, are committed to the total elimination of nuclear power technology through active involvement of large numbers of people in direct opposition to a technology that they explicitly characterize as capital

31

intensive and dependent on concentration of political power in hierarchical corporations and government agencies.

A critical plank in the philosophy of the direct-action groups is egalitarianism. Clams and Abalones see many of society's ills as deriving from hierarchical separation of decision makers from those who must implement decisions and bear their consequences. A driving imperative of their own organization is the creation and maintenance of strict equality among members with respect to group decision making. Egalitarian organizational principles are seen as challenging inequality in society as a whole. The emergence of publicly recognizable leaders, therefore, is strongly discouraged.

Although initiative is supposedly encouraged, individuals who take the initiative are frequently criticized for seizing power. The response of the Clams and Abalones to this problem has been the introduction of quite complex mechanisms for fulfilling the functions of leaders while preserving strict equality in decision making. Two such mechanisms are consensus decision making and the organization of affinity groups. The following description of these mechanisms is based on research carried out in 1980 (Riggs 1980). However, since then, public interest in nuclear energy issues has waned, and the groups have contracted, almost certainly resulting in some modifications to the structures and processes described below.

Consensus decision making requires a high level of participation in meetings. Although specialist committees or working groups met to plan and coordinate activities, they did not make policy decisions or initiate actions. These decisions required the participation of the whole group. However, even the specialist committees imitated the procedures used in meetings of the larger unit. In both the Clamshell and Abalone Alliances, meetings usually were led by a facilitator. This position generally rotated between all the members of the group who were prepared to do it, so the first item of business at each meeting often was to determine whose turn it should be to be the facilitator. The facilitator did not chair the meeting in the traditional sense, and there were no Roberts' Rules of Order. The facilitator's task was to help elicit opinions and encourage participation, not to determine the agenda or to resolve an impasse by casting vote.

Of course, de facto leaders did emerge. The same names kept cropping up on lists of contact people for various activities, especially on committees and in sub-groups. These were people whose commitment to routine work placed them in a position to make many practical decisions for the whole group. However, the requirement for achieving consensus on any major decision severely limited the opportunities for these individuals to establish and consolidate a position of overall leadership. The insistence on consensus decision making was designed to assure that individual rights were respected and that power was distributed evenly throughout the membership. The goal was to reach, without coercion or pressure, a decision upon which everyone could agree. The steps involved were described in an Abalone Alliance brochure:

- Gather information and different viewpoints
- Discuss possible outcomes and develop a proposal that will incorporate the best features of several ideas
- Check for objections or misgivings any members may have
- Alter the proposal until there are no more objections, or search for a new proposal.

This process of discussion, review, and revision could be extremely time consuming, and frequently hampered the effectiveness of the organizations. However, the benefits of consensus decision making were seen as outweighing these drawbacks.

Some local groups in the alliances, however, modified the idea of consensus to make it possible to reach decisions without complete unanimity. If no successful accommodation was made to a person's objections after a reasonable group effort, it was considered to be the individual's responsibility to examine whether the objection was really so strong as to justify blocking a decision. Of course, considerable peer pressure and normative pressure often was brought to bear on individuals to defer to the wishes of a substantial majority in the interests of solidarity and unity.

The direct-action groups bolstered their concern for equality and consensus with an emphasis on decentralization. The view of many anti-nuclear activists was that equality could be maintained only in small groups where personal contact is possible and no central authority can govern. They attributed much of the larger society's loss of concern for the individual to its centralization and consequent depersonalization. The development of a widespread but decentralized movement has, therefore, always been a goal of direct-action anti-nuclear groups.

An organization based on equality and decentralization has advantages beyond those of maintaining organizational purity and personal contact. The alliances explicitly recognized the advantages of what Gerlach (1971) has called polycephalous leadership. Particularly, they pointed to the difficulty opponents face in attempting to co-opt or destroy leadership when it is so diffuse. By discouraging the emergence of individual leaders, many activists aimed to guarantee the durability of the movement.

The Clamshell and Abalone Alliances coordinated major actions that required far greater commitments of time and money than the activities of local groups. Decisions about planning events, raising money, coordinating public relations, and establishing general priorities had to be made on an alliance-wide basis. To fulfill all of their organizational aims, the direct-action alliances attempted to maintain complete equality among members, remain as decentralized as possible, maintain mechanisms for decisions by consensus, and eschew sexism, authoritarianism and other societal patterns of domination. At the same time, they had to maintain organizations of several hundred members and coordinate activities that often involved thousands of participants. Many direct-action groups within the alliances attempted to resolve this dilemma by creating highly elaborate structures that defined how, and under what circumstances, decisions were to be made. The intent of these carefully devised structures was to maintain equality, prevent creeping centralization, and keep self-appointed leaders from making decisions for the organization.

The administrative structure of most direct-action groups was based on a system of collectives. This system was designed to solve the problem of dividing labor without admitting the legitimacy of leaders. Collectives were intended to be flexible - they changed as needs changed - and to provide a voluntary means of getting routine tasks performed by people who were willing to do them. Collectives performed a wide assortment of tasks. For example, in 1979, the San Francisco People Against Nuclear Power had over ten working collectives, including a media collective, an office collective, a non-violence training collective, and three finance-related collectives. In addition to this kind of administrative collective, most groups had collectives to organize specific projects. Member groups were urged to send representatives

34

to the various collectives, and individuals were free to join whatever collectives interested them.

This elaborate system of collectives and small groups was intended to allow a large alliance to continue making its decisions by consensus in small meetings. Most large groups and coalitions had detailed, and constantly changing, systems for representing the decisions of member groups and collectives in planning alliance-wide activities. In the Clamshell Alliance, for example, general decisions were made by a coordinating committee representing both the local groups and the other collectives. This served as a clearing house for decisions on how and when to have centralized actions, but no important decisions could be made without going back to the locals for consensus. Any major decision thus took at least two weeks, usually more, and required hours of discussion involving any member willing to participate.

Both the Clamshell and Abalone Alliances stressed the fact that their representative councils were intended to relay the decisions of member groups, not to make decisions for them. All decisions were supposed to represent the carefully solicited views of all members of each alliance. Leaders of any kind, even empowered representatives, were to be avoided at all costs.

During the planning and execution of civil disobedience, the collectives were augmented or supplanted by a system of affinity groups consciously modeled on the organization of the Iberian Anarchist Federation of the 1930s. Affinity groups were autonomous communal units usually composed of ten to twenty members who shared a common geographical or other affiliation. All of the participants of most occupations and blockades of the nuclear plant sites were members of affinity groups that often were formed during the non-violence training required before embarking on direct action.

In preparation for large demonstrations, the direct-action alliances stressed the importance of affinity groups, and even provided mechanisms for forming them in jail. Through these groups, the alliances were able to plan activities with thousands of participants and still retain a small-group communal structure. Each participant was protected from the depersonalization of the mob and given an equal voice in group decision making by his place in a small, communal group.

Affinity groups coordinated their decisions in much the same way as committees and member groups. Each affinity group had its own designated spokesperson or spoke, as in the connecting links of a wheel. The spoke represented the affinity group in the coordinating body, the hub of the wheel, as well as carried information back and forth between it and the affinity group. The spoke represented the opinions of his or her group and was required to report back to the group before the coordinating body reached new decisions. The role was literally one of spokesperson rather than an empowered representative.

Ideally, the decision-making body reached a consensus that represented the wishes of every member of each affinity group. Instead of being coordinated by a few leaders, demonstrations were managed by all participants. In practice, the system did not always work so smoothly. The problems of effective decision making during direct actions, such as occupations of reactor sites, are often incompatible with extreme democracy. The consensus process was enormously time consuming, especially when representatives had to run back and forth between committees and groups. Despite assurances that differences would be worked out and acceptable agreements would be reached, individuals or groups could block consensus. If people blocked consensus often enough, decisions were not made. Reports of meetings that were unable to reach agreement, or that spent hours discussing procedural questions were not unusual. One observer described a meeting during a demonstration at Seabrook where 'for at least an hour, they argued about what to discuss first.'

Rather than accept a hierarchy or limit their commitment to consensus, the direct-action alliances tried to increase the power of local groups and to decrease that of the central alliance. They advocated the formation of as many small groups as possible, and encouraged these groups to develop local concerns and to recruit local members. The groups might join together for large action, but they chose policy and made decisions on a local level. The alliances also tried to strengthen the power of affinity groups in a similar fashion. In both cases, the intention was to make the major unit of administration small enough to be governed communally.

One of the purposes of the direct-action alliances' carefully constructed coalition structure was to avoid schisms within alliances. When a group grew too large to make decisions communally it subdivided into component parts. Rather than growing until a major disagreement split the group, alliances thus tried to incorporate fission into their organizational structures. A number of separate groups united to form the Abalone Alliance. As the Alliance grew, it attracted too many new groups and individual members to retain its communal style and to guarantee everyone's participation in all decisions and activities. It, therefore, reorganized to ensure that decisions were made communally by local groups. Some of the local groups were still too large to ensure equal participation and therefore split into neighborhood groups.

The subdivision of direct-action alliances was largely successful in preventing major splits in groups. However, the alliances often were paralyzed by the inability of small member groups to agree on a course of action, though this paralysis rarely led to the establishment of competing splinter groups. Since local groups were expected to act on their own, they did not challenge the entire organization when they did so.

The recession in the strength and prominence of the direct-action alliances over the past half-decade seems to have resulted from a decline in interest in nuclear-power issues. No new plants are planned, and many under construction have been cancelled due to falling growth in electricity demand. The decline in direct-action groups does not seem to stem from organizational dysfunction.

Complex rules for the simple life

The rules for maintaining individual equality in the Abalone and Clamshell Alliances are every bit as expansive and detailed as those designed to ensure equality of treatment for factions in the IMG. They also impose high costs on the organization in consumption of resources, especially time and reduced instrumental effectiveness. However, both kinds of rules systems provide counter examples to the assumption, often made in evolutionary social theory, that egalitarian societies have simpler and fewer rules compared to those necessary to support hierarchical social organization. The equal-opportunity rules of the IMG and the strict-equality rules of the Abalone and Clamshell Alliances are complex, yet they are designed to promote equal access to decision making and preempt organizational frustration and consequent schism.

A solution to this apparent contradiction might reside in the concept of complexity itself. Gross (1983) has demonstrated how a mathematical model of complexity, conceived in abstract form by Kolmogorov (1965), applies to cultural patterns of activity. The Kolmogorov complexity of a sequence of mathematical symbols is defined to be the length of the shortest computer program that could produce such a sequence as its output. The most obvious computer program to produce such a sequence has one print instruction for each symbol in the sequence. However, it is usually possible to design a program with fewer instructions, if one permits the use of the programming constructs called 'loops' and 'subroutines.' Geertz (1973) commented earlier that there appeared to be a similarity between computer programs and cultural rules, and Gross showed exactly how to make such an interpretation. We might adopt Kolmogorov's usage for cultural analysis as the *expansiveness* meaning of complexity. Intuitively, this term refers to the minimum number of simple rules necessary to describe a system. This is a compromise of Kolmogorov's abstract system (designed for formal computer syntax) with a natural language, such as English, that is self-modifying.

A practical problem with Kolmogorov complexity, as Gross observes, is that no one has ever found an automatic method to produce, from a description of a rule, any computer program that faithfully represents the rule. (One way to interpret this is that no one knows how to replace all the computer programmers in the world by a computer program that does all their work.) Logicians not only have shown that this has not been done, but that it is impossible. Since the problem of writing the shortest program to represent a cultural rules system is much harder than the problem of just writing any program, it is no surprise that the Kolmogorov complexity of a rule system is implausibly difficult to calculate, except for very small rules systems.

As an alternative model for complexity of cultural rules systems, Gross proposed to use the Shannon (1948) information content, which is feasible to compute. It is difficult to give a complete, brief description of Shannon's model, but roughly speaking, the Shannon rank of a cultural rule system would depend largely upon the number of if-then entailments and the probabilities of the various cases. More precisely, the Shannon rank corresponds to the extent that the output of the process enables a sophisticated observer to infer the input.

According to this second view, complex systems are those with a high level of information, such that knowledge about the applicability of a rule to an individual case enables the observer to infer something else about that person or item. This may be described as the *intricacy* meaning of complexity.

It is important to note that an intricate system need not be expansive if the rules can be expressed concisely. Similarly, expansive rules systems, such as those that apply to decision making in both of the examples discussed in this paper, do not necessarily carry a high level of information that allows the observer to distinguish between individual roles or participants. To do that, we would need to be able to discover rules such as, 'The leader shall chair meetings.' These rules would allow us to make predictions like, 'If X is the leader, then X will chair the meeting,' or 'If X is chairing the meeting, then X is the leader.' Intricacy measures depend on non-substitutability of elements in a rules system; what were described in the introduction to this paper as differentiating or hierarchical rules. A system that is designed to promote substitutability has a low information content and is not intricate.

The examples of the IMG and the Clamshell and Abalone Alliances indicate that irrespective of whether egalitarian rules systems are defined as equal-opportunity rules (the IMG) or as strict-equality rules (the alliances), they always depend on maximizing the substitutability of membership elements (factions or individuals) in the decision process. Both kinds of rules systems are examples of low intricacy. Rules systems would be high in intricacy where they impose a specialized division of labor, especially one where entry is based on ascribed characteristics such as, gender, age, or social class.

The two case studies examined here indicate that, with respect to intricacy, the received wisdom of social science is quite justified in regarding egalitarian rules systems as being non-complex. However, the rules that maintain the substitutability of elements may be very complex in the expansiveness sense. We have seen how many rules are needed to maintain the low information content of activities with regard to status and leadership roles in both the IMG and the direct-action anti-nuclear alliances. The expansiveness of decision-making procedures in the IMG imposes heavy costs on members of large factions to the benefit of small ones. Similarly, decision making in the direct-action alliances imposes high temporal costs on all participants.

Confusion over egalitarianism and the complexity of rules systems seems to have stemmed, at least partly, from our failure to discriminate between intricacy and expansiveness. Thus, some societies with expansive rules systems for decision making may have been accused unjustly of concealing hierarchy. Moreover, those societies with few, but effective, differentiating rules may have been successful in preserving an undeservedly egalitarian reputation (Mars, this volume). Certainly, it must now be clear that the establishment of customary rules for decision making does not, of itself, lead to routinized inequality. On the contrary, expansive rules for ensuring low intricacy may be designed and enforced precisely to undercut existing hierarchy, or to prevent one from emerging. The iron law of oligarchy turns out to be a little more flexible than Michels (1915) allowed, and more a question of societal choice about organizational principles than a natural and inevitable process of bureaucratization.

Unlike the distinction between equal-opportunity rules and strict-equality rules, the enlarged concept of complexity provides a consistent basis for evaluating egalitarianism. My suggestion is that by developing the concepts of intricacy and expansiveness of rules systems, we can provide ourselves with the means to make relative measures, on an ordinal scale with some kind of metric, that would provide consistent criteria for making judgements about the topics discussed in this entire collection of papers. I am speaking of equality, hierarchy, and access to decision making. These issues are fundamental to any society that depends on the consent of its members, as is especially the case with voluntary organizations. Unless the rules are seen to be fair, all, or part, of the membership will withdraw its consent, and the group will split. Of course, in other contexts, fairness is not synonymous with equality and non-egalitarian groups would insist that fairness must take into account factors such as varying degrees of effort and proportional rewards. However, these fairness criteria are not compatible with the strict-egalitarian preference for equality of condition and substitutability of basic organizational units, whether these units are factions or individuals.

Bibliography

Bennett, John W. 1967. *Hutterian Brethren.* Stanford, California: Stanford University Press.

Douglas, Mary 1978. *Cultural Bias.* Occasional Paper 35, Royal Anthropological Institute, London.

Geertz, Clifford 1973. *The Interpretation of Cultures.* New York: Basic Books.

Gerlach, Luther P. 1971. 'Movements of Revolutionary Change: Some Structural Characteristics.' In *American Behavioral Scientist* 4:812-36.

Gross, Jonathan L. 1983. 'Information-Theoretic Scales for Measuring Cultural Rule Systems.' In *Sociological Methodology 1983-1984* (ed) S. Leinhardt. San Francisco: Jossey-Bass.

Hirschman, Albert O. 1970. *Exit, Voice and Loyalty.* Cambridge, Massachusetts: Harvard University Press.

Kolmogorov, A. N. 1965. 'Three Approaches to the Quantitative Definition of Information.' (In Russian). In *Problemy Peredachi Informatsii* 1:3-11.

Michels, Robert 1915. *Political Parties: A Sociological Study of the Oligarchical Tendencies of Modern Democracy.* New York: Hearst.

O'Hare, Michael 1977. 'Not On My Block You Don't.' In *Public Policy* 25:407.

Olson, Mancur 1965. *The Logic of Collective Action.* Cambridge, Massachusetts: Harvard University Press.

Rayner, Steve 1986. 'The Politics of Schism: Routinization and Social Control in the International Socialists/Socialist Workers' Party.' In *Power, Action and Belief* (ed) John Law. Sociological Review Monograph 32, London: Routledge and Kegan Paul.

Rayner, Steve 1982. 'The Perception of Time and Space in Egalitarian Sects: A Millenarian Cosmology.' In *Essays in the Sociology of Perception* (ed) Mary Douglas. London: Routledge and Kegan Paul.

Rayner, Steve 1979. 'The Classification and Dynamics of Sectarian Forms of Organization.' PhD Thesis, University of London.

Riggs, Katherine 1980. 'Anti-Nuclear Groups: The Goals, Tactics, and Composition of the American Anti-Nuclear Movement.' Center for Survey Research, Berkeley, California.

Schulze, William D. 1980. 'Ethics, Economics and the Value of Safety.' In *Societal Risk Assessment: How Safe is Safe Enough?* (eds) R.C. Schwing and W.A. Albers. New York: Plenum Press.

Schumann, Hans Wolfgang 1973. *Buddhism*. London: Rider.

Shannon, C. E. 1948. 'A Mathematical Theory of Communication.' *Bell System Technical Journal*, 27.

Wildavsky, Aaron 1984. *The Nursing Father: Moses as a Political Leader*. Birmingham, Alabama: University of Alabama Press.

3 Egalitarianism or solidarity in Basque industrial cooperatives: the FAGOR Group of Mondragón

DAVYDD GREENWOOD

ABSTRACT

In the famous labor-managed Mondragón cooperatives, an egalitarian ethic coexists with manufacturing systems involving a complex division of labor, educational differences, and social complementarities. Explanations of the cooperatives' success often center on egalitarian elements in Basque culture, including a 'democratic' regional government and equality in agrarian sex roles. Based on research by other scholars and on fieldwork, the paper argues that the Mondragón cooperatives are done a disservice by this 'mythic' picture, and emphasizes instead the complex interdependencies of hierarchy and equality within these industrial organizations.

The focus of this paper is a discussion of the diverse effects of the polar typology - equality/hierarchy - on external analyses of the FAGOR Group of labor-managed cooperatives in Mondragón (Guipúzcoa) in the Spanish Basque Country, and an analysis of the members' very different vision of the cooperatives.[1] For outside analysts, the assumed contradiction between hierarchy and equality must be resolved in favor of equality in the cooperatives. With this resolution, the cooperatives are seen to be egalitarian organizations whose success offers hope for the future of industrial democracy.

Cooperative members' own sense of the character and importance of their cooperatives centers on economic profitability and social solidarity rather than equality and the future of democracy. While they share outsiders' concerns about hierarchy, insiders' attention to optimal economic performance and their lack of appetite for general social equality is overlooked in external analyses. This oversight occurs partly because outside analysts often are committed to furthering industrial democracy, and assume that cooperative members share a commitment to larger-scale social reform.

To capture these dimensions, the paper expands the discussion of the issues of equality and hierarchy in the cooperatives to include the crucial concept of solidarity. It also shows the lack of fit between internal and external views of the essential features of the Mondragón cooperatives, and how insiders and outsiders to Mondragón appeal to their own deterministic versions of the equality/hierarchy polarity to explain the labor-managed cooperatives' success.

The case

The case study[2] centers on a group of 13 cooperatives forming the FAGOR Group. FAGOR is a subgroup of the more than 161 labor-managed producers' cooperatives located in the Spanish Basque town of Mondragón (Arrasate[3]) in the Province of Guipuzcoa. These industrial and service cooperatives were started by a small group of local men in 1956 under the guidance of a local priest, Don José Maria Arizmendiarreta.[4]

When Don José Maria arrived in 1941, Mondragón was a poor mountain town with about 9,000 inhabitants, including 1,500 mental patients in the nearby asylum of Santa Agueda. The asylum was located in the buildings that used to house one of Spain's most famous nineteenth-century mineral water spas.

The Basque Country is one of the most densely populated and highly industrialized regions of Spain. Once famous for its blast furnaces and shipbuilding industry, it suffers from the same decline in these sectors that is experienced in most parts of the world. Now it is a region of intense manufacturing activity, high per capita income, extensive immigration from other regions, and high unemployment. About 23% of the population has immigrated from regions in Spain outside of the Basque Country. Unemployment stands at a startling 27% of the work force.

Noted as the birthplace of Charles V's chronicler, Esteban de Garibay, and as the source of blades for Toledo swords, in the first half of the twentieth century, Mondragón lived primarily from small industrial operations and the surrounding agricultural economy. Employment was scarce, educational opportunities limited, and emigration a constant fact.

Don José Maria had come to Mondragón after the Spanish Civil War to take up his pastoral responsibilities. Influenced by the ideas of Catholic Action, and strongly committed to social betterment, he began by improving the local school system, particularly in the area of professional education. He wanted the youth of Mondragón to have a better chance to earn a living, and at the same time, he inculcated in them the ideas of democracy in the workplace. From these classes, the first founders of the cooperatives were drawn. Since that time, the school system he started has expanded and sub-divided into an enormous array of technical and business-education programs, including university-level instruction.

The history of these cooperatives is well told in a variety of publications (Azurmendi, 1984; Gutiérrez Johnson and Whyte, 1977; Larrañaga, 1981; Oakeshott, 1973; and Whyte and Whyte, forthcoming). A group of Arizmendiarreta's students from his Professional School attempted to reform the working conditions in existing local industries and failed. After this, and under his guidance, they decided on a separate course of action, and sought permission to manufacture small stoves under a foreign patent license. Overcoming a number of important obstacles with Don José Maria's help, they established the first labor-managed industrial cooperative, ULGOR in 1956. The name is a composite of the names of the founders. From this simple beginning, the vast Mondragón cooperative network quickly grew, despite a complex web of legal impediments about the corporate structure permitted for cooperatives, and by the 1960's, ULGOR had become a major force in the white-line appliance market in Spain.

Along with this success, came two other crucial developments in the history of the cooperatives. In 1958, a national ruling prohibited cooperatives from participation in the national system of worker's compensation and social security. The members of ULGOR were forced to develop their own insurance system. The result was the creation of a so-called 'second order' cooperative, Lagun Aro, that provides health insurance, unemployment insurance, and retirement pensions. Its benefits are more comprehensive than those provided by the national system, and its relative costs of operation are lower. Then, in 1959, Don José Maria convinced the cooperators that the key to their long-term survival was fiscal independence. He encouraged them to create a small savings and loan association, Caja Laboral Popular, that also was organized as a cooperative. The creation of Caja Laboral was a turning point because it quickly became one of the most important savings and loans in the north of Spain, providing the capital and financial knowhow to permit the continued expansion of the cooperative movement.

Since then, the cooperatives have grown at an unprecedented rate, and now number more than 161 with a total of over 16,000 laborer-owners and an engineering consulting cooperative (Ikerlan). The cooperatives employ about half the workforce in the region where Mondragón is located (the Alto Deva), and they have captured an increasing portion of Spain's national and export market. Their annual rate of growth in sales averaged 30% in the 1960s and 8% in the 1970s. Exports were 18% of total sales in 1979, and the target figure for 1985 was 30%. The cooperatives generally outperformed their competitors in the market by a very substantial margin.[5]

The cooperatives manufacture a wide variety of items: electrical appliances, industrial robots, cabling systems, computer circuit boards, metal castings, furniture, and many more. The system also contains a large and highly prosperous supermarket chain.

The membership process is begun by applying for a job. If the application is successful, the worker begins on a probationary status and must pay an entrance fee, which is approximately the equivalent of a year's salary. This sum may be worked off over the first few years of employment in the system. After a couple of years, assuming acceptable performance, the worker becomes a permanent member.

Each year, the next year's costs of operations are laid out for the members, and investment plans are agreed upon. These capital requirements are subtracted from the profits, and the remainder is distributed to the members in direct compensation and in shares. Thus the worker-owners largely capitalize the operations themselves.

The organizational structure of a typical cooperative can be diagrammed as follows:

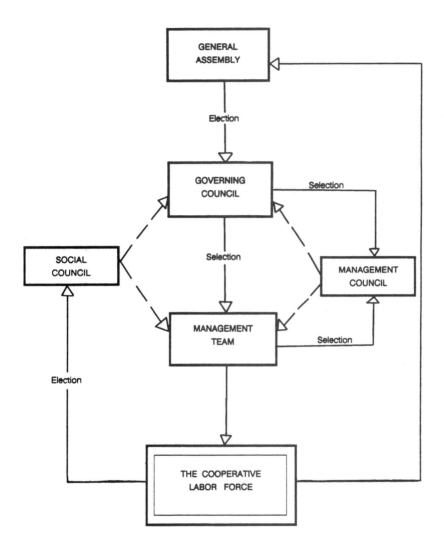

Figure 3.1 The organizational structure of a typical cooperative[6]

Ultimate control rests with the General Assembly of all the members. From among the members, the Junta Rectora (Governing Council) is elected, which in turn selects the Management Team for a four-year term of office. Junta Rectora and the Management Team nominate a Management Council that oversees the managerial operations of the cooperative. The Social Council, elected from the members at large, serves in a day-to-day advisory and watchdog capacity.

Independent cooperatives are linked directly to Lagun Aro, Caja Laboral Popular, and the technical assistance cooperative (Ikerlan). Many of these cooperatives are linked to each other in cooperative groups; the FAGOR Group is the largest, containing 13 cooperatives, a total of 6,000 members, and ULGOR, the first Mondragón cooperative. The FAGOR Group has its own central management division and central services, so that, while linked to the other second level service cooperatives, FAGOR provides many infrastructural services directly to its own cooperatives.

Throughout the cooperative system, the compensation scale is officially set at 1:3, meaning that the highest paid members receive only three times the amount of the lowest paid.[7] Compensation at the lower end of the job classification is keyed to the average wage in the region for unskilled labor. In practice, virtually no one receives compensation as low as 1.0; the lowest paid are currently receiving 1.6. A very small number of members receive 4.5. Thus the effective ratio is actually less than 1:3. This is a remarkably flat compensation scale, one that gives the high-level managers compensation and benefit packages far below what they could command outside of the cooperatives.

Within the cooperatives, social services are superior to those found in private industry, and members are guaranteed employment. While unemployment in the Basque Country currently hovers around 27%, throughout their history, the cooperatives have never laid off a member. Following this principle during the recession of the 1980s cost all the members a considerable amount of money. On occasion, people have been shifted from one cooperative to another, sometimes at the cost of personal trauma, but jobs have never been lost. Thus, the lower echelons come to the cooperatives and stay, because the pay is good and employment is secure.

The willingness of highly sophisticated executives in internationally competitive industries to work under the continual scrutiny of all cooperative members, under the threat of immediate censure and even recall, while earning much less money than their colleagues in other regions, seems puzzling. Many of these executives have received offers of significantly higher salaries in non-cooperative firms throughout Spain, yet none have gone.

In part, they stay because they are fervent believers in the cooperative movement; indeed, to become cooperative leaders, they must have consistently exhibited such belief. While it is possible to attribute such motives to the substitution of high status gains for high income, this explanation does not quite get at the experiential dimension of leadership here.

Though it is true that business leaders are generally respected, a key element in the cooperative conception of leadership is service. To rise within the system means acceptance of increased self-sacrifice, albeit in return for respect. Thus, while leaders are given the right to lead, and are expected to do so, this authority is purchased at the cost of their total commitment to the cooperatives, including a willingness to forego the extra income that could be earned elsewhere for themselves and their families.

Leaders are also products of the cooperatives, rising within the organizations by performing many different jobs in them. They are known for, and elected because of, their success in embodying cooperative ideals and leadership style. For them to leave such an environment, after achieving success within it, would be to transform their entire style of life and move into an utterly different social environment. It is not surprising that few find this step attractive.

These cooperatives are unique within the Spanish socio-economic system. Although legislation favorable to cooperatives exists and has been effectively used by the Mondragón cooperatives, labor-managed industrial cooperatives are uncommon. Their level of economic performance, combined with their unusual socio-economic structure, has made them a famous case both within Spain and outside it.

Standard external explanations

The explanatory approaches in previous studies reveal a desire to explain away Mondragón, either by making the cooperatives unique and impossible to imitate or by arguing that if the same conditions that were present at the founding of the Mondragón cooperatives existed elsewhere, similar cooperatives could have arisen. Either way, Mondragón disappears as an explanatory problem.

Three basic explanatory approaches have been used. One focuses on racial/ethnic/cultural factors; another stresses economic factors in the local industrial environment; and a third argues that ethical behavior in business is rewarded by success. A brief review of these strategies will show how they serve to make the Mondragón case disappear as a theoretical problem. This review also helps clear the way for a review of the cooperators' own analysis of what is most important about Mondragón.

Racial/ethnic/cultural factors

In the work of authors like Oakeshott (1973),[8] economic factors play an important role when posed against a cultural and historical background. As such analyses portray this background, they generally emphasize the following characteristics: the unique Basque language, the history of Basque nationalism, the religiosity of the Basques, the role of Don José Maria, the prevalence of egalitarian drinking groups, and the historical Basque industrial tradition.

Few anthropologists would denigrate the importance of cultural factors in social history, and this is certainly not my intention. But different ways of handling cultural factors have very different explanatory consequences. In most explanations of the cooperatives, these cultural factors are treated as uncaused, static givens in the local situation that, in turn, explain why the cooperatives emerged in Mondragón. Rather than serving as the beginning of an analysis, this 'cultural' approach fends off analysis by simply saying that the cooperatives are the direct expression of universal, fixed characteristics of Basque culture. The historically dynamic character of these cultural features, their variability among populations, the presence and importance of the 25% immigrant population in the cooperatives are cast aside.

The Basque language cannot be used to explain the cooperatives. The language, unrelated to any other language currently spoken in the world and a rallying point for the Basque nationalists, is not spoken at all by more than a quarter of the members and is distributed over the whole Basque Country. Since the cooperatives are not distributed over the same area, the language cannot explain their existence.

The relationship between the cooperatives and the Basque nationalist movement is most complex. There is no single Basque nationalist movement, but rather a shifting array of political embodiments of a political agenda that is not itself precisely defined. There are some separatists who advocate the creation of an independent Basque Country, but the vast majority supports varieties of home rule provisions permitting free expression of Basque culture within a federated Spanish state. Among this group, there is a wide variety of political options.

The cooperatives do not have a clear political color. The Spanish market was and is vital to their economic interests. Non-Basque immigrants have formed a large and important part of the work force and management of the cooperatives for at least two decades. Divergent views over the proper approach to regional politics has done as much to divide the membership as to unite it. Further, the Basque nationalist movement encompasses the whole Basque Country, but the cooperatives began only in Mondragón. Thus Basque nationalism does not explain the success of the cooperatives.

References to Basque religiosity raise issues that would require a longer treatment. It is true that the Basque Country was heavily influenced by Jansenism, and thus, Basques can find support in Catholicism for a strong work ethic. It is also true that some segments of the Church enjoyed more solidarity with their parishioners in various periods of civil strife in Spain than was the case in many other regions.

Ethical values bearing a strong Catholic stamp are vitally important in the organization and operation of the cooperatives, but Basque religiosity explains little by itself. Religiosity, however one would measure it, is distributed all over the Basque Country, while some of the most active members of the cooperatives are profoundly anti-clerical.

The role of the founder is undoubtedly very important. It raises the vexing issues that have always surrounded the hero in history: is it the great man who creates the circumstances or the circumstances that create the great man? Don José Maria is a peculiar charismatic leader. A poor public speaker and an often opaque and tendentious writer, he convinced his followers by the force of his ideas and personal example. Perhaps his particular genius lay in incarnating Catholic ethical values in practical institutional forms, in dealing with the endless array of legal and institutional matters without losing sight of his larger social goals of democracy and self-realization through work (Azurmendi, 1984; Larrañaga, 1981).

Overemphasis on the role of Don José Maria leads to a romantic image of the cooperative past, of the founding of a fully formed and perfect cooperative idea in 1956. A closer look shows that the initial conception of the cooperatives was neither very clear nor did it seem very promising. The success of the cooperatives arises from their ability, and that of new generations of members, to use the basic idea to develop the institutional structures, and to try to embody more fully over time the kind of industrial democracy that was only vaguely conceived in the 1950s. Thus, the cooperatives were not born complete in the mind of a founding genius. His role was important, but the cooperatives are a social product of the efforts of thousands of members.

Among other things, Don José Maria founded the schools, and many members of the cooperatives are graduates. While it is tempting to think that the cooperative schools play a crucial role in forming and supporting cooperative values, this does not appear to be so. Though a proper assessment of this notion would require a close study of the vast school complex, it appears that educators concentrate on a very standard curriculum. The schools offer a high-quality education, not the inculcation of cooperative values.

Much is made in the literature of egalitarian drinking groups in the Basque Country. This social phenomenon is important generally throughout the region. It centers on a group of men who stroll from bar to bar together after work, snacking and having a glass of wine. Not only are these groups stable, but they tend to be composed of people from different social classes. While this is interesting and tells us something important about Basque ideologies regarding social class, it is not possible to erect an explanation of the cooperatives on the interclass solidarity of egalitarian drinking groups, especially since these groups are found everywhere in the Basque Country and in many other parts of Spain.

Finally, appeals are made to the Basque industrial tradition as an explanation for the readiness of the people to succeed in business. While there was an industrial tradition in the Basque Country, it was modest. It began with the small forges whose ruins dot the landscape and whose activities denuded the country of hardwoods; later, it included an active shipbuilding industry and the Bilbao ironworks. It is not clear what this has to do with the cooperatives. These industries were not centered on Mondragón, were not particularly well organized or successful, and showed none of the social concerns embodied in the cooperatives.

Thus, explanations that involve culture as a just-so story cannot withstand scrutiny. They rest on homogenized and romanticized visions of the Basque past, and confound more than they clarify. To the extent that they apply at all, they apply to the whole Basque Country, making it impossible to explain why the cooperatives only developed in Mondragón. Treating culture as a fixed repertoire of characteristics does violence to the complexity and dynamism of all cultural systems.

Often, all of these cultural features are mentioned together, and so rapidly, that the reader is left with the impression that while no single feature explains the cooperatives, together they do. But this is surely wrong. Taken together, five inaccurate explanations of Mondragón are simply five inaccurate explanations.

Yet, elements of Basque culture are certainly relevant to the cooperatives. Egalitarianism, literacy, respect for laws, etc. interact in important ways with the cooperative movement, and they must be dealt with in any attempt to understand the trajectory of the cooperatives. As global causal explanations, however, these elements are clearly insufficient.

This limited view also contains an extremely negative political lesson for those who would wish to treat the Mondragón cooperatives as a model for imitation. If the success of the movement is based on unique features of Basque culture and history, then outside imitation is a forlorn proposition, at least without the imposition of Basque cultural repertoires on non-Basque groups. The message of this kind of cultural analysis rapidly becomes the following: the Mondragón case is not a theoretical or practical challenge. It is idiosyncratic, just as the Basques and the Spaniards are idiosyncratic. Thus, this mythic picture at once idealizes Mondragón and isolates it.

Economic analyses of cooperative success

Few would pay attention to the Mondragón cooperatives were it not for their economic success. The suggestion that democratic, cooperative organizations can compete successfully in a plural economy both stimulates imitation and undercuts those who justify the unfairness of capitalist society as an inherent characteristic. For this reason, authors who focus almost exclusively on the economic determinants of the success of the Mondragón cooperatives are numerous. Among these, Thomas and Logan (1983) provide the most detailed analysis of the economic performance of the cooperatives. Their valuable work merits a close reading.

Thomas and Logan devote a considerable portion of their work to posing and answering the theoretical question; 'Are the cooperatives *genuine* examples of labor self-management?' After referring to the theoretical literature on labor-managed systems and reviewing the requisite characteristics of a labor-managed firm, they study the characteristics and performance of Mondragón against this backdrop to determine if the cooperatives are truly labor-managed cooperatives. They conclude that the Mondragón cooperatives pass the definitional test, and, therefore, are worth studying in detail.

Thomas and Logan develop a detailed and useful economic analysis through which the reader gets a good sense of the mode of operation of the cooperatives. Despite the effort they put forward, Thomas and Logan state their conclusions in a very passive form: there is no a priori reason not to try this model elsewhere. In other words, the local economic conditions are not so unusual that they make the Mondragón model completely irrelevant in another location. Put the other way around, the cooperatives are seen to conform to the tenets of general economic theory, and, therefore, may be taken seriously.

Eclectic views

Elements of both cultural and economic explanations are combined in works like Bradley and Gelb's *Cooperation at Work: The Mondragón Experience* (1983). Advocating cooperatives as a component in a pluralistic capitalist system, they see them as a response and partial solution to the general problems of advanced capitalism. According to them, this creative response was possible in Mondragón for a variety of reasons, and these authors partly reproduce the arguments about local cultural features already discussed above. In addition, they argue that class conflict is weak in the Basque Country; that Mondragón is a small community, and therefore able to create solidarity; and that the isolation of the Spanish economy from external competition during the formative years made the cooperatives possible.

While attention to the socioeconomic context of the cooperatives is certainly reasonable, the empirical bases for these assertions are not easily established. While it is true that the public idiom of class conflict is muted in the Basque Country, it is not true that class conflict is weak. And to speak of a comparative measure of class conflict would require theoretical specification that is quite daunting.

The assertion that small communities create solidarity flies in the face of generations of anthropological research showing that small communities can create solidarity, conflict, and usually some combination of both. Scale alone is insufficient as an explanation.

Their point about the isolation of the Spanish economy during the formative years certainly deserves more consideration and development. It may well be that in a perverse way, the isolation of Spain created by the Franco regime and the international arrangements that permitted and supported Franco's continuation, actually created something of a captive market for Mondragón's early products. However, the Spanish market was open to all of Spain and certainly to all of the Basque Country. Why did Mondragón take advantage of the situation and not other communities?

Taken together, such analyses do not really clarify the lessons of the Mondragón cooperatives and their potential transfer elsewhere. A combination of idiosyncratic cultural and economic features is used to explain why cooperatives like these have not arisen elsewhere. At the same time, much of the analysis seeks to prove that nothing about Mondragón conflicts with general economic and social theory. Thus, the analyses move inconclusively from a focus on the idiosyncracies of Mondragón to the general laws of culture and economy.

Whatever the explanatory strategy adopted, previous analyses share an unproblematic sense that the members are strongly committed to egalitarian ideals. This is felt to be so clear that much time is spent examining the evidence of remaining hierarchy within the cooperatives only to show that their great success has not yet entirely eradicated hierarchy. The message is generally intended to be one of hope, that Mondragón, like all human inventions, is imperfect. And, like all human inventions, it is potentially replicable in other places.

Outside writers are generally interested in the cooperatives because of a shared concern with furthering democratic values in industrial society. To this end, some views of Mondragón argue that the cooperatives have succeeded because industrial democracy will prevail if taken seriously. Mondragón is taken to prove that capitalist industrial production and democratic ethics can support each other, and that the evils of capitalism are not intrinsic to the system, but are the results of failure to seek democratic alternatives within the capitalist system.

Taken together, the literature on the cooperatives charts an ambivalent course. The works tell a good deal about the ethical standards and theoretical predispositions of the authors, but do not offer much clarification about the aims and wishes of the cooperators themselves. Among the most important features lost in this way are the members' overarching concern with the profitability of the cooperatives and their acceptance of hierarchy as a necessary principle in industrial organization. But hierarchy can only be tolerated when mediated by social solidarity.

Egalitarianism in the cooperatives

It is generally agreed that the cooperatives of Mondragón are egalitarian in fundamental ways. This universal perception is at odds with what members say, with much of what I observed in the cooperatives, and with the daily experience of most of the members. Yet, from an external vantage point, the cooperatives are genuinely egalitarian. Rightly impressed by the flat compensation scale, the election and potential recall of managers, the Social Councils, the consultative character of decision making, commitment to one set of rules for all, and to protection of the interests of all the members, outside observers characterize the cooperatives as highly egalitarian.

For members, however, the concept of egalitarianism has little resonance. In interviews and roundtables conducted from February to July, 1986, members at all levels refused to employ the term equality, preferring instead to speak of solidarity when analyzing the aims of cooperation. Equality for them is a vacuous empirical assertion because it overlooks individual differences in capacity, effort, and interest. It also seems that they see equality as a concept that stresses the individual over society. Thus, insiders and outsiders have a different view of industrial democracy.

56

In thinking about the cooperatives in terms of solidarity, insiders emphasize the social character of the cooperatives. The aim and emphasis of cooperation is to create a solidary social system in which all individuals are treated fairly, but no amount of solidarity will create equality. As they look at the problems the cooperatives face, members center first on economic viability and then on a concern with and fear about the persistence of hierarchical relationships.

However, outside observers must not interpret this concern with hierarchy as a desire for an egalitarian society. Rather, the issue is to be certain that mobility through effort is possible, and that the relations of production be, first and foremost, human relationships that offer all individuals personal dignity in the workplace.

It is essential to approach such questions with definitional clarity. Generations of social research have made it clear that hierarchy and equality are relative terms, not simple descriptions of concrete social forms. Social differentiation is an ingredient, but not the only one. As with most relational terms, as the point of comparison shifts, the meaning alters.

As insiders and outsiders to Mondragón interact with each other and think about the cooperatives, there are considerable opportunities for confusion, for dialogues in which both sides use the same words but do not communicate, or in which neither side truly listens to the other.

The frame of reference and vantage point of the speaker must be specified. For members, relevant comparisons are with non-cooperative industries in Spain and with their ideals for what the cooperatives could truly be. When they compare themselves with non-cooperative industries, they stress economic performance, employment security, and the opportunity to have an impact on the course of events. When they respond to questions by articulating their ideals about cooperatives, they then are extremely critical of the persistence of hierarchical authority structures and threats to individual dignity created by excessively technocratic management strategies.

Within the cooperatives, no one speaks of equality. Even Don José Maria did not argue that equality was the organizing principle of the cooperatives. He spoke of dignity, liberty, democracy, and self-realization, but he did not see the cooperatives as an attempt to create social equality. In our recent interviews and roundtables, none of the respondents saw equality as an important dimension of the cooperatives.

They insisted that the goal of the cooperatives was the genesis and maintenance of social solidarity among people of different talents and social classes. Nearly all appeared to accept the notion that people have different capabilities and levels of commitment to the cooperatives, and that they should be compensated differently. They did insist, however, that every member is equally deserving of proper social treatment and respect.

The members accept the idea that the very structure of industrial production requires a complex division of labor in which workers with different skills cannot serve as substitutable elements, systems of control, or a division of management and production activities. Certainly they do not believe that hierarchy necessarily must be as extreme as it is in many cases, but they realize that some degree of differentiation and hierarchy is inevitable. Further, the cooperators themselves strongly believe that those who take on major responsibility for the operation of the system deserve to be compensated for their efforts and recognized for their contributions.

Thus, the compensation structure is a hierarchical one with a formal classification of jobs that determines the level of compensation the workers receive. A great deal of effort was and is expended on classifying jobs according to this scale and generally tailoring the operations of the system to take account of these differences. Curiously, the size of the differences that separate jobs on this scale is very small when compared with nearby industries. Thus, the Mondragón system seems to provide extremely egalitarian rewards by any national or international standard. This situation gives rise to outside feeling that the cooperatives are radically egalitarian.

At the same time, throughout their history, the cooperatives have seen debates about the compensation structure and its fairness. When there was a reclassification of jobs across the board, a complex methodology was used for the purpose. The classification process involved a study of the job itself and its evaluation by a point system according to a set of criteria agreed upon by the members. It resulted in raising some jobs in the classification and lowering others. A complex grievance system was then set in motion for people to appeal any job classification that they felt was unfair. This process was accompanied by some conflict, though it was ultimately successful.

Rather than focusing on hierarchy as a problem, the members are much more concerned about the character and tone of human relationships within the cooperatives. They do not wish to abolish authority structure; they want authority to be exercised without authoritarianism. As members, they expect their elected managers and middle management to treat subordinates as functionally subordinate, but humanly equal. Thus, solidarity for insiders is both a belief about ultimate human equality and a requirement for a management style that respects all individuals.

In the view of many members, this ideal of solidarity is often violated in the course of daily operations in the cooperatives; subordinates are sometimes treated in an imperious manner, and are not fully informed of the reasons for orders given. The increasing scale of the cooperatives and the use of technocratic control systems threaten not the equality but the solidarity of the cooperatives that many members view as their essential feature.

Yet, the same members also caution us and themselves not to take the analysis to extremes when they compare the cooperatives with ordinary capitalist firms. Their own perception of non-cooperative industries is that worker-management relations are far worse there, because workers can be fired and must follow orders without question. They told us repeatedly that most people joined the cooperatives, not because of a commitment to industrial democracy, but because jobs are scarce, and because, once in, a member is guaranteed employment. Only after being in the cooperatives for a time do some members begin to become interested in and committed to cooperative principles.

Members are aware that they have many means of express-ing their views. They can vote in the General Assembly, they elect the Juntas and Social Council, they lobby their represen-tatives, and they can directly express their views to manage-ment. All major issues, including the annual business plan, changes in the bylaws, complaints about management errors, etc., are dealt with in meetings to which the general member-ship has access. In addition, the information about the structure and economic operation of the cooperatives that is available to members is mindboggling. Basically, the books are open to all.

In the abortive strike of 1974, an event that still resonates in today's discussions, one of the issues at stake was the notion that one set of rules had to apply to all members. The strike, initiated by a minority of workers after they had exhausted all the normal procedures for getting majority support for their particular position, was seen as an attempt to have special rules made for one group of people.

This attempt was rejected as an attack on the solidarity of the cooperatives because it suggested that different rules should be applied to some groups within the system, without sufficient reason for the exception. The anti-strike position argued that sufficient internal institutional recourse existed to deal with grievances of any group, and the strike was an example of a minority imposing its will on a majority. Subsequently, the strikers were expelled by a vote of the membership, though later they were offered readmission to the cooperatives, and most returned.

Since 1980, the cooperatives have struggled to deal with the worldwide recession. The policies adopted required a great deal of debate and discussion, and have had costs for everyone in the system. The recession policies underline the cooperatives' solidarity in guaranteeing employment security, moving managers into production line positions where needed, and in recalling top managers when they could not cope with the problems for the benefit of all.

Outside observers often compare the cooperatives with an abstract model of the capitalist firm. From this vantage point, the cooperatives are egalitarian, as the above examples show. However, if the comparison is made with cooperatives worldwide using some sort of ideal-typical hierarchy/equality continuum, Mondragón's acceptance of hierarchical staff structures and compensation systems would place the cooperatives toward the hierarchical end. At the same time, outside observers' quite reasonable emphasis on egalitarianism obscures the complex and ambivalent views on egalitarianism and solidarity held by cooperative members themselves.

Inside and outside views compared

The various pieces fit together in a complex way. Insiders are troubled by hierarchy within the cooperatives, particularly against the background of their ideals for proper forms of social interaction within a cooperative. They accept hierarchical structures of jobs and authority, but worry that this kind of structure can get out of hand. At the same time, they see the cooperatives as more solidary than capitalist enterprises, and they value highly their standing as members.

Outsiders find it difficult at first to perceive the existence of hierarchy and to credit members' active concerns about it, because, in a worldwide frame of reference, the cooperatives are quite egalitarian. We are intrigued to note that the distances between each decimal point in the job classification system - almost invisible to those of us accustomed to looking at ordinary business and administrative systems - are seen in the cooperatives as very great gaps. From 1.6 to 1.9 on the scale is seen as a major distance, and the subtle distinctions that are made and maintained show how it is culturally possible to create complex differentiations that are intensely lived, even though they are so small that outsiders have a difficult time even perceiving them.

The cooperators well know, especially those who came to the cooperatives after working in ordinary businesses, that the Mondragón cooperatives are more egalitarian than other local industries. Further, these other businesses are on shaky economic ground, and workers are regularly laid off or even terminated without much notice or consideration. Until recently, labor unions were illegal, and there was little or no job security. Benefits were regularly not paid, and insurance coverages were poor and unreliable. Observers must not forget that in a country with over 20% unemployment, in a region in which that figure is higher, and in a valley where the lack of jobs in the past led to persistent emigration, having a secure job is a great social good in itself.

An outside observer's sense of the cooperatives' egalitarian structure is also troubled by the members' acceptance of a hierarchical job classification system and the lack of insistence on more purely egalitarian forms of organization, i.e. equality of condition. The intensity of their concern with decimal points in the classification system centers, not on the abolition of hierarchy, but on fairness and clarity of the rules by which the classifications are made. It is logically coherent for members to argue about the classification system and yet to accept hierarchy, while outside observers easily confuse the concern with the classifications with a repudiation of hierarchy itself.

As a result, in some contexts, the members and outsiders experience the cooperatives as egalitarian or solidary, and in others, as hierarchical and conflictive. The point of reference may shift, and the same person may see the same organization in two different ways almost simultaneously.

Are the cooperatives of Mondragón egalitarian or hierarchical?

By now it should be clear that this question can only be dealt with in relation to a specified frame of reference. There can be little doubt that the cooperatives are characterized by a good deal of social differentiation. Like all industrial organizations, they operate via a division of labor that is both technologically and operationally based. Though one of the cooperatives is experimenting with a redesign of the assembly line that is intended to create greater solidarity in work groups, the basic production processes in Mondragón differ little from those found elsewhere. These processes involve the creation of differentiated jobs and complex command and control structures.

This 'normal' degree of hierarchy is intensely experienced by a few people working in the system who see it as a defect to overcome, but most members do not attribute much importance to the continued existence of hierarchy. Rather, everyone worries that the authoritarian habits of ordinary industry will invade the cooperatives and eventually do away with them. Thus, every new initiative is scrutinized for its implications in regard to authority and social solidarity.

At the same time, the cooperatives have achieved a startling degree of equality/solidarity within production systems that are supposed to be very hostile to this. Many members experience the cooperatives as solidary and feel that they are part of one of the most promising experiments in industrial democracy ever. For them, the Mondragón cooperatives are highly participatory by comparison to outside businesses within Spain and around the world. The high degree of participation is evident in the compensation levels, the almost complete self-financing of the operations by the members, and the complex of committees and councils that regulate the internal operations and set the collective goals. One of the key dimensions of this participation is the commitment to a common social ethic; a commitment to deliver the same non-monetary benefits to all members.

If the focus is shifted from social structure to process and rules of conduct, the picture takes on other dimensions. One virtual constant in discussions with members is their unshakable commitment to one set of rules of the game for all. From this vantage point, what makes members equal is not that they do the same things or make the same contributions, but that they are all subject to the advantages and disadvantages created by one set of rules. The extraordinary commitment to rules and processes that encourages participation is a hallmark of the system.

In many respects, this insistence on the same standards for all workers is a key element in the solidarity that so many members value more than equality; no one is above the rules. While assembly-line workers are subject to many rules and requirements, some imposed without the development of a social consensus, being subject to the rules is a condition shared by all members. The CEO and other elected managers are subject to member censure and to recall, and such recalls and censures have occurred in the history of the cooperatives. No one is above the rules, not even those founders who are still active in the cooperatives.

Equality also is found in access to services provided by the cooperative system itself. Members are guaranteed employment security; all have access to the educational institutions that the cooperatives either directly sponsor or have founded over the years. The cooperative social security system and its benefits are available to all.

All members can participate in the governance of the cooperatives. Virtually anyone with a desire to play an active role can do so, though being elected to some of the councils obviously depends on gaining the support of fellow members. Attendance is taken at General Assembly meetings, and those absent without a valid excuse are not permitted to vote at the next meeting. At the same time, members believe that cooperation is a social attitude that cannot be legislated. Cooperatives must be run in such a way that people actively want to participate. While everyone has an opportunity to participate, the sense of obligation ultimately must come from the individual. If enough individuals fail to participate, this is taken as an indictment of the quality of management of the cooperative. For insiders, so long as a significant portion of talented people participate, they see the cooperatives as healthy.

Outside observers, if they place a stricter construction on the idea of a cooperative, may see the lack of broader member activism as an indication of problems within. They may emphasize the degree to which a relatively small number of highly active individuals continually refashion the rules and move the cooperatives along, with the apparently passive acquiescence of the broad membership.

Which of these realities is the real one? Clearly both are real and relevant. The inside and outside views refer to different points of comparison, and are reasonable to the extent that they do not demand the reduction of the cooperatives to one or another view. The distance between participants and outsiders in experience, interests, and aims cannot be reduced by positivist sleight of hand that privileges the investigator's own frame of reference over all else. The social forms of the cooperatives are real and definable; insiders' and outsiders' different subjective experiences of them are also real.

Conclusions

The interplay between internal and external perspectives analyzed in this paper permits both a rendering of some of the characteristics of the Mondragón cooperatives and the exploration of a variety of meanings of egalitarianism. It also provides resources for a critique of the deficiencies of a strictly positivist perspective in the social sciences. It shows that the polar typology, hierarchy/equality, held differently in the minds of cooperative members and social researchers, itself is an important part of the reality of the cooperatives. This, in turn, argues that linking strong modes of cultural analysis with the study of political economy is essential.

One particularly confusing element in the analyses of the cooperatives of Mondragón is a failure to distinguish between at least two widely understood meanings of egalitarianism. The members of the cooperatives actively reject the term equality as applied to their organizational structures and aims. They strongly emphasize solidarity, by which they mean a commitment to one set of social rules for all members and a style of interpersonal relations that asserts the equal worth of individuals at any level of the organization. They then can point to a variety of institutional mechanisms and contrasts with outside organizations that supports this vision. They worry about hierarchy in the system, not because hierarchy itself is unacceptable, but because it is easy for hierarchy to become authoritarian rather than solidary. They want everyone in the system to have an equal right to participate, to be considered as a human being with dignity. But they go one step farther. The system of sharing profits and losses and member financing of production means that, after the race is run, the outcomes are also equalized according to the hierarchy of the job classification system.

In the United States, we, too, have a commitment to egalitarianism. Though culturally real, this commitment is quite different from that found in Mondragón. We actively argue for equality of opportunity, not for solidarity in the sense in which it is sought in Mondragón. We do not demand that we must live here and now in an egalitarian system, and we tolerate hierarchy without much discomfort, except in moments when fervor for democratic ideals arises. We accommodate and even admire the successes of others, because we conceptualize equality as equality of opportunity, and attribute the inequalities in our society to the differential striving and/or intelligence of the people within the system. Our ambivalence about welfare policies and affirmative action programs tells us that we like to think about equality as an equal start in the race, but not as an equalized outcome at the finish line. For us, the persistence of inequality does not threaten our egalitarian commitments.

The irreconcilability of the external and internal visions of the cooperatives is not a sign of a failure of analysis or of a defective theoretical model. The differing frames of reference, each having its own foundation in social structure and cultural meanings, do not compete, but render different facets of the same reality.

The cooperatives of Mondragón also depend culturally on the world of non-cooperatives for their existence. The members' vision of the hierarchical world outside the cooperatives heavily influenced the founding and organization of the groups as well as the members' continuing commitment to them. The larger social context in which the cooperatives developed, and to which they are self-consciously counterposed, are a fundamental part of their reality. Mondragón is intended to be an alternative model within the capitalist system, an embodied critique of capitalist relations of production.

So it is with the outsiders' vision of Mondragón. Heavily influenced by a perception of capitalist society, the structure of industry, and the range of alternatives available, outsiders in part construct Mondragón out of their beliefs about the human condition in capitalist society. We draw comparisons using materials from outside of the experience of the members of the cooperatives, and justify acting or not in the world outside of Mondragón partly by counterposing Mondragón to ordinary reality as we understand it.

These views are neither valid nor invalid because they are ours rather than theirs; they are simply different. The divergence between inside and outside views must be understood for what it is. All statements about other societies are comparative; we can only choose to make explicit or implicit comparisons. So long as our comparisons remain implicit, a host of the implications of social experiences like those of Mondragón will be lost to us.

Notes

[1] The research reported on in this paper is a preliminary result of a two year project carried out between the FAGOR Group of the Mondragón cooperatives and Cornell University with support from the Joint Committee on Education and Cultural Affairs of the U.S./Spain Treaty of Friendship and Cooperation. Their active support of the project is gratefully acknowledged.

This article has benefited greatly from the generous comments and criticisms of James Flanagan, Peter McClelland, Steve Rayner, and William Foote Whyte.

[2] Most of the analysis presented here results from a joint effort in participatory action research between Cornell University and the Personnel Department of Departamentos Centrales of the FAGOR Group of cooperatives. The co-directors for Cornell are William Foote Whyte and Davydd Greenwood, and for FAGOR, José Luis González. Centering on participatory action research in the cooperatives, the project is an attempt to better understand the cooperatives as a dynamic process and to develop internal capacity in the central Personnel Department to carry on social research. The core group of six and a shifting team of some twenty people has actively participated in the project since February, 1985.

One of the aims and emerging outcomes of this participatory action research process has been to mediate the differences between outside and inside views of the cooperatives. Through active collaboration and extended debate, we have come to develop a perspective that blends the interests and concerns of both parties. This combined vantage point is the basis for what follows.

The project has a dual agenda. One purpose is to demonstrate that the cooperatives are a process, not a fixed recipe. They are dynamic and innovative, and have only survived because they are highly adaptable. The second agenda is to enhance the ability of the staff of the Central Personnel Office to conduct effective social research in service of their general mission as a personnel department. They describe the cooperatives as a socio-economic process, and are seeking to match the sophistication of their economic planning models and strategies with their social planning and interventions.

67

[3] Arrasate is the Basque name for Mondragón. Both names are in current use in the area.

[4] An excellent introduction to the ideas of Arizmendiarreta is that recently published by Azurmendi in 1984.

[5] These figures come from Bradley and Gelb (1983), p.14.

[6] This figure is a simplified version of that found in Bradley and Gelb, 1985, p. 38.

[7] I call this compensation rather than salary to come closer to the Spanish word used in the cooperatives, *anticipo*. The compensation package for the year is set by anticipating what the profits for the next year will be. This amount is then meted out according to the compensation scale, and any additional amount is returned to the members in the form of shares in the cooperative. If the profits are below the level set by the compensation scale, the shortfall is proportionally distributed across the membership.

[8] Oakeshott initiates the public interest in the cooperatives and is sincerely impressed with their performance. He has an enduring commitment to the potential of cooperatives in advanced industrial economies, and wrote about Mondragon in service of that ideal. I am critical of the consequences of his analysis, not of his motives. I am also treating it as one of a number of analyses that rely on the same approach to the analysis of cultural dimensions of the cooperatives, including all those works mentioned below.

Bibliography

Azurmendi, Joxe 1984. *El hombre cooperativo: pensamiento de Arizmendiarreta.* Mondragón: Caja Laboral Popular.

Bradley, K. and A. Gelb 1983. *Cooperatives at Work: The Mondragón Experience.* London: Heinmann.

Bradley, K. and A. Gelb 1985. *Cooperativas en marcha: el caso Mondragón.* Translated by Jordi Beltran Ferrer. Barcelona: Ediciones Ariel.

González, José Luis and Davydd Greenwood (eds) n.d. *Learning from Reality: Participatory Action Research in the FAGOR Group Cooperatives of Mondragón.* In preparation.

Gutiérrez Johnson, Ana and William Foote Whyte 1977. 'The Mondragón System of Worker Production Cooperatives.' In *Industrial and Labor Relations Review*, Vol. 31, No. 1:18-30.

Larrañaga, Jesús 1981. *Buscando un camino.* Danona, Oyarzun.

Oakeshott, R. 1973. 'Mondragón, Spain's Oasis of Democracy.' In *The Observer*, January 21:44-47.

Thomas, H. and C. Logan 1983. *Mondragón: An Economic Analysis.* Boston, G. Allen & Unwin.

Whyte, William Foote and Kathleen King Whyte n.d. *The Making of Mondragón: Building the Basque Cooperative Complex.* ILR Press, forthcoming.

4 Rules, rulers, and ruled in egalitarian collectives: deviance and social control in cooperatives

STUART HENRY

ABSTRACT

Drawing on interview and participant observation data from a number of housing, worker, and consumer cooperatives in England, this paper will examine the way that egalitarian collectives establish and enforce primary rules and principles for shaping and controlling their members' behavior. These methods will be discussed with respect to the way the egalitarian ideal of informal collective justice often relies on, and is used in conjunction with, more formal, elitist, and rationalist forms of social control. The nature of this contradiction is explored and explained in terms of the cooperatives' interdependence with both human agents and the wider capitalist structure in which the cooperatives are set.

Introduction

In the literature on and practice of collective organization, there is considerable debate about how egalitarian a collective can be when set in the context of a capitalist society. Many of the issues relate to attempts by collectives to distance themselves from contamination by the non-collectivist ideology and structure of capitalist society. Thus, core issues are:

how to avoid hierarchy; whether specialization is inevitably undermining; how to prevent cliques; how to maintain commitment and full participation; whether differential reward systems are always undesirable; what relations to have with non-collective structures; and what to do about uncooperative members such as the free rider.

Much can be learned about this whole range of issues by focusing on the last. The way an organization deals with its deviants can tell us about its internal social structure and operational practices. In this paper, I shall take an analytical approach developed by sociologists and criminologists for theorizing about law, crime, and criminal justice (Young 1981; King 1981), and apply this to the rules, deviance, and discipline found in the evidence on a variety of cooperatives existing within British capitalist society.[1]

The analytical framework will consider six interrelated dimensions of the collectives' disciplinary system.

- First, I will discuss the view of human nature taken by advocates and members of collectives. The key issue here is whether people are basically socially responsible or whether they are naturally differentiated.

- Second, I will examine the view taken of social order within the collective. Central to this issue is whether the division of labor and occupational specialization necessarily imply hierarchy.

- Third will be a discussion of the nature of rules in cooperatives and, in particular, whether these are always informal, spontaneously created, and diffusely applied, or whether there are also occasions where formalization and legalism take precedence.

- Fourth, I will discuss the perspectives that collectives take toward rule breaking and deviance. Here it is important to resolve the question of whether deviance is seen as individualized or as part of the wider relations of disputing within the collective. Also important are the views taken by cooperatives about the cause or causes of their members' deviance.

- Fifth will be a description of the procedures used by cooperatives for administering discipline and justice. As with a discussion of rules, it is important to look at whether procedures are always informal and collectively administered, or whether they are

71

sometimes formal, administered by elite groups, or even by individuals.

- Finally, I will examine the philosophy of sanctioning used by cooperatives to enforce their rules. I will try to determine whether this is designed to celebrate the individual rule breaker as an indicator of the need for organizational growth, to encourage the individual's reform, or whether the moral condemnation such as shaming, ridicule, and ostracism are used to deter unacceptable behavior.

The last section of the paper will draw the analysis together with a discussion of why egalitarian collective structures in capitalist society are constantly being undermined. I argue that the recurring trend toward dissolution of collectives has to do with the way the wider social structure permeates, but does not wholly determine, the social forms that emerge within it.

Of vital importance to any discussion of deviance and discipline is a consideration of the way individual human agents are perceived and of the organizational structure in which they are seen as acting. I will begin by looking at the view of human nature and social order taken by advocates of collective structures. This will be juxtaposed with evidence taken from my study of cooperatives before I go on to discuss the dimensions relating to deviance, discipline, and justice.

The view of human nature

Some commentators on cooperative behavior have pointed to its utilitarian roots while others have taken a pessimistic view of human nature (Olson 1965). However, advocates of social cooperation are more optimistic about it being an essential human trait. For Marx, humans are intrinsically social agents, potentially open to development and change under the right structural conditions (Geras 1983). They are fundamentally social beings who create the world in which they live, but not under conditions they have chosen for themselves; 'Rather on terms immediately existing, given and handed down to them' (Marx 1852:115). An even more radically individualist position was taken by Proudhon (1876) who viewed the cooperative human spirit as secreted within a person, imminent, constituting not only human essence but the essence of society itself.

These arguments need not imply that humans are identical. My study of cooperatives found a common belief that humans were separate individuals with different personalities, abilities, and interests. Some were seen as having strong personalities, others weak ones, and these personalities could clash. This view was reflected in the weight many cooperatives gave to procedures of selection that were designed, in part, to match personalities. Some cooperatives even placed matching as a priority over shared principles and ideology. For example, a member of an electronics commune said, 'You must work towards being a community of friends rather than being a community of like-minded people.' But even with such procedures, people develop differences.

> Although in theory we are very much a coop of equals, I do think we inevitably move away from this ideal. But only within limits that are quite acceptable, because we are all different people.

Moreover, people's qualities are not seen as fixed, but open to change through their relations with others. There is, said the above cooperative member, 'a continual process of relating to somebody, and there are inevitable changes in the relationship which occur as you live with them.' Such change is possible because of the human qualities of reflexivity about oneself and sensitivity to others to whom we relate and with whom we can empathize.

The view of social order

The view of social order taken by advocates of cooperative organization is coalescent with their view of human nature. For Kropotkin, 'man... was not naturally solitary... He was naturally social and his natural form of social organization is that based on voluntary co-operation' (Woodcock 1977:18). Indeed, the freedom of individuals, argues Wieck (1978:230), is 'defined not by rights and liberties but by the functioning of society as a network of voluntary co-operation,' such that order is 'constituted freely through manifold agreements, contracts, negotiation.' This view flows from the nature of human agents choosing voluntarily to cooperate, and results in a society composed of a plurality of organic groups.

A central idea of this view of social order is that government should be decentralized, with the emphasis being placed on face-to-face contacts and shared decision making among all of its members. 'Each group is to be small enough that all members know each other,' and size should be such that people can 'relate to one another in a variety of ways' (Gaus and Chapman 1978:xxxiv). This, it is argued, leads to the strengthening of connecting bonds between people and the elimination of the alienation that accrues from impersonal structures that emphasize separation and fragmentation. As a member of a community farm whom I interviewed said,

> We have all known each other for quite a long time and all of us also live together in a cooperative situation. It's our close relationship that largely accounts for our commitment and lack of serious disagreement. Because we know and trust and respect one another's feelings about a situation, we take each other into consideration and make as much effort as possible to accommodate one another and make allowances, real disagreement rarely occurs.

Woodcock (1977:22) says that in a collective structure of the kind we have been considering, decision-making authority begins among individuals and small groups: 'The most important unit of society... is that in which people co-operate directly to fulfill their immediate needs. Nobody can assess these better than those that experience them.'

A crucial issue here is whether the authority for decision making resides in the individual or the group/collective. Some, such as Rothschild-Whitt (1979:509), argue that authority resides not in the individual but in the collective:

> Decisions become authoritative in collective organiza-tions to the extent that they derive from a process in which all members have the right to full and equal participation... there is a 'consensus process' in which all the members participate in the *collective* formula-tion of problems and negotiation of decisions... All major policy decisions are decided by the collective as a whole. Only decisions which appear to carry the consensus of the group behind them, carry the weight of moral authority... are taken as binding and legiti-mate... Ultimate authority is based in the collective as a whole, not in the individual.

Indeed, although decision theory has been invoked to show how collective decisions differ from the sum of individual inputs and may have unintended outcomes, the notion that collectives make decisions is open to the charge of reification. Collectives are abstract constructs that merely appear to make decisions; beneath the appearance is the reality that only individuals can make decisions because only individuals have human agency. Moreover, though these decisions intermesh and also have unintended consequences, there are no grounds for attributing the choice to an abstraction.

This agency-based view recognizes that individuals are free within the collective structure to deliberate in the exercise of their own responsibility on an equal basis with fellow members, but it does not simultaneously deny their agency by expropriating it to an abstraction. Thus, in contrast to Rothschild-Whitt, Ritter (1978:132) argues that,

> the one most crucial... justification of authority is their commitment to the overriding value of rational deliberation, understood as choosing and acting on the basis of evidence and arguments that one has evaluated for oneself.

He argues that only when individuals have freely exercised their own authority can the process of sharing individual decisions begin. From such sharing derives the consensus: 'All members of society must exercise authority before its directives can deserve support' (Ritter 1978:135, 1980).

In spite of these ideals, the cooperatives in my study did not always achieve the desired consensus through egalitarian decision making. As well as the exploitation of the collective structure by powerful individuals, I found confirmation of Olson's (1965) observation that the weak also were able to exploit the strong.

Demonstration of the first case can be seen in the comments of a member of an electronics commune who said, 'Even if you think you've got a consensus system... people with the strongest personalities so often carry everyone else with them; it's almost as if they are able to control the direction in which we go.' The ability for some to exploit the collective structure was also illustrated by a member of a theatre collective who said:

> If we look at a meeting which is deciding an ideological move, someone... will be able to say, 'Yeah, Cliff is the one who usually speaks about these things. We often find ourselves agreeing with him.' Of course, all sorts of factors operate on it... experience,

competency in speaking and social skills in manipulating situations, which I have, for instance. All these things are going to predetermine the decision in a particular direction and usually it works in Cliff's favor.

A member of an arts collective captured the essence of this exploitative ability when he confessed to me that, 'In two and a half years I've learnt how to manipulate these meetings. I've learnt how to do lots of horrible things.'

Some members of collectives believe that the very institution of the meeting actually encourages exploitation by the more powerful. As a member of a housing cooperative told me: 'there's an element of listening to the sound of your own voice... the joy of getting a point over and the feeling that you're getting something done.' For others, the meeting is seen as facilitating gender relations of power, as the following account from a member of an electronics commune shows:

> One could postulate that meetings are sexist... The men seem to enjoy meetings as a sort of social interaction, a bit like being down at the pub together or boys in the back room, and it's quite a strong interaction for them... The women are stronger in terms of one-to-one interaction in the course of the ordinary productive process... Both are methods... to find out what other people are thinking about, to express your own opinions, interact and through that, make decisions. But if you're then going to say 'meetings are how this coop makes its decisions,' it may be that there is a sexual bias to it.

Some members believe that the tendency for a minority to rule stems from allowing individual differences to be used as a resource. This is subsequently enhanced by specialization that itself develops into hierarchy. According to Rothschild-Whitt (1979:517), in order to avoid such a development some cooperatives 'aim to eliminate the division of labor that separates intellectual workers from manual workers, administrative tasks from performance tasks,' by creating a series of generalized jobs, holistic roles and non-specialized functions. As in many communal structures (Rayner and Mars, this volume), this is achieved through job rotation, internal education, and task sharing.

However, not all agree that a division of labor is necessarily detrimental, nor that it inevitably means hierarchy (Unger 1975). As Gaus and Chapman (1978:xxxv) argue,

> The purpose of occupational specialization is to foster development of some aspects of men's many-sided selves to the fullest possible extent. Specialization promotes romantic expression... Thus respect for human differences is preserved without... domination.

Indeed, in the cooperatives I studied, this view was evident, as reflected in the comments of the following member of a wholefood collective:

> Most of the... alternative society people that... we associate ourselves with think that the essential thing about a cooperative is that nobody really tells anybody else what to do; that every decision is not just collective but sort of consensus; that you don't vote on anything; you are all able to do everything. But these, to me, aren't the essential ingredients of a cooperative... I'm beginning to question whether they are even realistic or feasible... Look, what are the aims of a cooperative enterprise? A democratic structure... in which everyone is accountable where any profits... are distributed amongst the workers... but not necessarily a structure in which every single person has exactly equal responsibilities.

The above view, coupled with the ideas that individuals are different in personality, competency, and interests, leads to the kind of imbalance in decision making that I have been discussing. But this does not mean that division of labor, specialization, and inequitable decision making inevitably divides experience. As a member of a theatre collective said:

> For Greg, who is learning about performing, to interest himself in the details of administration would destroy his ability to perform... Geoffrey is a far more interesting artist than me... It is important that we have posters that are good rather than posters that I have learned a lot doing... Therefore, Geoffrey is... the obvious choice to do the posters. It's clearly a division of labor... But I don't think this necessarily means a division of experience. Nor does it imply hierarchy... I think to experience a process in a real way is to experience an intelligent selection of... little experiences. The essential experience is the one

which is built up to, in our case, creating a show and the experience of getting it out on the road.

Although less immediately obvious, examples of Olson's exploitation of the strong by the weak are also evident in my findings. Later, we shall see dramatic examples of how individuals can invoke the wider societal structure, and the way that members subjected to disciplinary action by the collective can invert any intimidation by the group to maximize their own interests. For the present, the basic point can be illustrated from the following case of a housing cooperative. Here, the exit costs of members deciding to leave a meeting were low enough to make coercion impossible by those who decided to stay:

> In an important general meeting... people just happened to be wandering out. You know they were going home to their tea or something and the finger was pointed: 'These people are leaving the meeting. Isn't it a disgrace?' Well, there was no evidence to suggest that they were acting in the wrong way, and they took offence. They said 'Fuck you!' and left.

At a broader level of analysis, whether the basic unit of a collective society is described as the parish, commune, workshop, cooperative, or collective, the links between this unit and others is typically envisaged as administrative rather than governmental. The work place or neighborhood is the vital nucleus of social life, and associations formed around these arenas of interaction federate loosely, where they have interests in common, to discuss ways to cooperate and to arbitrate differences. 'The whole world becomes a federation of federations of federations, bringing together every small community in a kind of symbiotic unity like a great structure of coral' (Woodcock 1977:26). This is not to say, of course, that there are not splits and divisions, but these, as we shall see, later may be seen as constructive growth enabling the collective to survive in a changing environment.

Rules and deviance

According to scholars who have theorized about the nature of rules in decentralized collective structures, these rules are designed to reflect both the interests of the sum of individual members and to serve consensually agreed goals. The rules cannot be constructed by anyone other than those whose interests they directly affect, since only the person subject to possible harm knows how much of that risk he wishes to absorb and how much he wishes to control. Abel (1982:702), for example, argues that risk control is best achieved through a cooperative structure in which each person is 'able to control the risk to which he or she is exposed' and where people share equally, 'those risks we collectively choose to encounter' (Abel 1982:710).

Nor can the rules be fixed in advance or written down, since, in the ideal structure, there should be no limits on spontaneous decision making, because this is the only guarantee that members are always fully responsible decision makers. Indeed, for Unger (1976:202-3), all who have 'communitarian aspirations... will look for an alternative to legality in the notion of a community bound by shared experience and capable of developing its own self-revising customs or principles of interaction.' Similarly, for Rothschild-Whitt (1979:513), 'No written manual of rules and procedures exists in most collectives, though norms of participation clearly obtain.'

It is important to recognize here that there are exceptions to these characterizations of rules in collective structures. While it was generally the case in the cooperatives I studied that most imperatives were in the form of informal norms that were subject to change, other essential principles were quite inflexible. There were also occasions where attempts were made to fix rules by having them written down, however, more than not, these attempts were resisted. Although oral rules can still be formal, the symbolic refusal to write them down left members relatively free to deliberate and take responsibility for their actions.

The speakers in the following quotations discuss a concern in their housing cooperative about the failure of some members to take responsibility and participate in day-to-day management activities. The intention was to introduce formal rules as part of a more formalized disciplinary policy. The quotations illustrate both the kinds of rules that cooperative members take to be important and how formalization can be resisted by the members:

> So we put together this motion: 'Every member of the coop shall assign themselves to one predetermined area of work in List A within which their skills may lie, and can be called upon to utilize their skills and assist in running the coop. Anyone who persistently

fails to help when asked will have their membership questioned by the participation sub-committee (that was to be set up if the motion passed). In addition, no member shall be exempt from assisting in any area of activity in List B.'

But... it was amended. Someone got up and said, 'I'll support anything so long as there is no compulsion in it.' He was a very good speaker. The part about the compulsion and about being checked up on by a participation sub-committee got fought against and we lost it. It was dropped.

However, the relative absence of formal rules does not, it must be emphasized, deny the existence of informal rules governing activities taken to be deviant, as we shall see later. Indeed, the labeling of some behaviors as deviant is itself a reflection of these informal rules and norms.

What counts as deviance is that which offends the collective interests, irrespective of whether or not a specific rule has been broken. At a general level, 'The abuse of persons and anything that tends toward creating patterns of "enslavement" or that hinders the realization and continuity of free coopera-tion is wrong in such a society' (Wieck 1978:232). Behavior that goes against the cooperative spirit of taking full respon-sibility for one's actions in a socially aware way is considered deviant. It includes any number of specific actions and can be called by any member of the cooperative; indeed, not to call attention to deviance would itself be seen as avoidance of responsibility and may invoke its own questions.

Concrete examples of rule-breaking behavior, as we see from the above cases of attempts to have them controlled, are: failure to participate in activities of the cooperative such as meetings; unwillingness to help other members if asked; attempting to create personal advantage at the expense of other members; and failure to contribute an equal amount of effort. Indeed, as Taylor (1982:120-23) states in his review of communes and other intentional communities, 'a central problem was inequality of work effort.' Free riding in any structure where benefits are available on the basis of need or on an equal basis, independent of contribution, is tantamount to theft (Olson 1965).

The cause of such behavior is attributed to individuals themselves, since they and they alone are responsible for their action. At the same time it is recognized that any particular incident may be the outcome of the shared responsibility of all rather than being the responsibility of one individual. It is such a position that leads to the celebration of deviance, since other members of the collective can take responsibility for their contribution to the nonconstructive behavior, as I shall discuss later.

Procedures for administering justice and discipline

Gurvitch (1947), like Ehrlich (1913) long before him, pointed out that in any social structure or substructure, it is possible to discern a number of levels of formality whereby control is administered. This is no different for collective structures such as cooperatives. Some commentators, however, have tried to generalize about decision making in collectives. Schwartz (1954:476) for example, has said that decision making in kibbutzim, 'must be considered informal rather than legal.' Similarly, Rothschild-Whitt (1979:513) has observed, 'Decisions ... tend to be conducted in an ad hoc manner... are generally settled as the case arises, and are suited to the peculiarities of the particular case.'

The cooperatives in my study certainly showed evidence of a preference for informal procedures. As a member of the electronics commune said,

> We have got rules about how people could be asked to leave... but I can't imagine that we'd ever resort to them. It would be very much seen as a last resort... By the time things had got that far, that the majority of the people didn't want somebody living there, they'd already have got the message.

At its most informal level, the disciplinary process was part of the ongoing relations of commitment and concern felt by members of the cooperative for each other. The approach involved handling offenses continuously in the course of everyday working and interaction. It involves, as Godwin observed in the 18th century, the 'inspection of every man over the conduct of his neighbors' (Woodcock 1962:83-4). For one member of a housing cooperative whom I interviewed, 'The cooperative spirit is actually doing the right thing without the formality,' that, for members of the electronics commune, took the form of open discussion:

> We have evolved mechanisms for preventing disciplinary problems... All the time I'm asking them what they think about the standard of what I'm doing. There is a group feeling that we should do this.

> We have no supervision as such and find that the best form of control is by our fellow work mates in the same group and through open discussion with criticisms of each other in as constructive a way as possible.

Part of the reason such continuing criticism is possible is because the cooperative is not fragmented into isolated parts: 'Most of us are working and living together, so it doesn't happen that we have anybody who is socially isolated. Because of that it is much easier to discuss problems.'

But procedures are not limited to purely informal, face-to-face messages. When disturbing behavior is not adequately controlled through the informal process, an organized forum focuses members' attention more sharply (Schwartz 1957, Rosner 1973). The deviant can be reminded of his duties and responsibilities at a formal group meeting 'by drawing his attention to the implications of his action for other coop members and for himself, personally.' Because of the close-knit nature of cooperative relations, reminding a housing cooperative member, for example, that he is in arrears with his rent can be a powerful inducement to reform: 'If his friends are there, there is much more pressure to pay... group pressure.'

Importantly, not all deviants in cooperative organizations submit meekly to the collective sentiment. Some use the collective structure as a resource to exploit the cooperative's softer side whilst avoiding its harsher controls. One astute member of a housing cooperative, for example, accounted for his lack of attendance and non-payment of rent as a result of personal and emotional difficulties stemming from unemployment in the wider capitalist structure, and invited the caring cooperative to reconsider its policy of collective justice. In response to questions about his rent arrears he exclaimed:

> Look, I'm shit scared! It's sheer hell to stand up and explain your financial expenses to a meeting of twenty or thirty people. This coop policy just frightens people who are already in a state about their inability to pay, who are unemployed and on social security.

As another member of the same cooperative said, collective justice,

> puts people on edge to be strong about it. It's
> incredibly humiliating and I think it's a cheek to
> make people come along and be humiliated, because I
> don't think it's going to make them want to be more
> cooperative. It's just going to put their backs up.

This ability of the relatively powerless individual to turn the collective policy against the collective can pose severe control problems for the cooperative. As a member of the same housing cooperative explained:

> None of us wants to get our fingers burned or be
> seen to be being heavy, so what happens? We'd be
> nice to them and make an arrangement for them to
> pay. We'd start feeling sorry for them. 'Ah poor
> dears. They've got all these problems. Let's make it
> easier for them... Perhaps we ought to restructure the
> coop to make it more accessible!'

As another said of a notorious problem member: 'People think "Oh, he's got a lot of problems!" But it's only because we know about his problems, because he's made damn sure everybody knows about them.' A member of a wholefood cooperative similarly pointed out that, apart from being bad from the financial side, such exploitation of collective justice can have a very negative effect on morale: 'Because everyone believes in being nice to everyone, one person can put a complete spanner in the works.'

In the context of collective justice, it is, as Olson (1965) has observed, almost as if the harder the sanctioning mechanism, the more powerful are the resources available to the individual being sanctioned. A good illustration of this is to be found in the use by some cooperatives of disciplinary subcommittees in which, as Schwartz found, specialized functionaries are 'delegated the task of intra-group control' (Schwartz 1954:473).

Although seemingly against the principles of collective justice, specialized functionaries are sometimes deemed necessary, as when members of a housing cooperative neither pay their rent nor attend meetings to explain why. Clearly the whole collective cannot visit en masse, so a subgroup might be invited to volunteer. Although a very intimidating technique, sensitivity to this fact ironically renders the cooperative vulnerable to further exploitation by the individual. For example, at one of the regular meetings of a housing cooperative that I attended, there was a lot of self-conscious humor and joking about how the visits might be seen. One member asked: 'What's it going to be then, a knee job?.' Another replied: 'They're not going to break his legs, just bruise him a little - where it can't be seen!'

While the visits system can produce a range of responses from the deviant member, these tend toward extremes. A member of the visits committee told me that 'one girl in particular was taken aback and abusive.' He said that, 'If there isn't hostility, then the person being visited is bound to get overwhelmed.' Cooperative members are very aware that 'It is intimidating when six people suddenly descend on you with no prior notice... It's not a good forum to discuss personal things like, "Are you going to pay your rent?" and "Why are you not paying it?".' It is no easier for those visiting. 'It freaked me out,' said one member. 'We went as a group of six and stood around shuffling our feet, feeling very uncomfortable.'

It should be pointed out that, in the cooperatives I studied, this ability for the individual to turn the collective pressure back on the cooperative was not restricted to occasions of hostile reception. Even where the visitors were invited into the member's home, a surprising amount of power could be reflected back onto the visiting committee. There were usually not enough seats for six or so people arriving unannounced. Even if there were, the visiting party was so sensitive to its intimidating appearance that it was easily disarmed by questions about fellow cooperative comrades, friendly offers of hospitality, and apologies. The quicker the subject of rent arrears could be dropped and leaving rituals begun, the better everyone felt.

By driving a wedge between those exercising control and the rest of the cooperative, this institution of subcommittee discipline can actually escalate the problem. For example, where the deviance is the not uncommon practice of a member failing to participate, the act of collectively disciplining that person can result in the deviant feeling even less involved and being less willing to participate. This, in turn, can result in an even greater control problem for the collective.

Subcommittee discipline is also vulnerable to the charge of personal vindictiveness. As a member of a housing cooperative said: 'The individuals concerned are surprised and resentful when they see a comrade knocking on the door. Quite a lot react aggressively... feel they have to hit back. People think they are victimized.' Indeed, by the nature of cooperatives, nearly all members know each other quite intimately, so where one group acts to discipline a fellow member, resentment is often inevitable. One ex-member of an arts collective, for example, said that her own expulsion 'was rigged all the way through by these people - this particular woman who wanted me out. She'd got a lever through her husband to every committee.'

Perhaps the ultimate irony is that, in order to resolve these kinds of difficulties, some cooperatives have sought to eliminate personal feelings from their control policy by resorting to the outside legal system to support their collective disciplinary action. A member of a housing cooperative explained that after the visits system had caused a number of inter-personal disputes within the cooperative, and some members were still avoiding paying their rent, a different approach was adopted:

> You see, the problem when you're trying to use discipline or just logic is that people get in the way. To run an efficient rent system you've got to get the human element out as much as possible because that's what messes the whole thing up - people's emotions... So that's why we introduced the new system. Now if they're four weeks behind with their rent they get a warning letter; if they're eight weeks behind they get a notice to quit, and when that expires we take court proceedings. Of course, the main objection is 'Oh that's a bit heavy getting the law involved.' We are allowing the police to harass our members... but there's no option. You just have to kick them out.

Although Ritter (1978:138) has claimed that the kind of authority that underlies the cooperative enterprise, 'being intimate, particular and internal, cannot issue directives of a legal sort,' clearly my evidence supports the argument of Shapiro (1976) who suggests that this tendency to legalism co-exists with informal procedures. Both serve to bring together those who offend and those who are offended to resolve their differences. As Shapiro (1976:429) says:

> The possibility that the kibbutz will not prevent the initiation of police action... has a subtle influence in strengthening internal controls in the kibbutz. This

parallels the way tribal societies use the colonial power to strengthen traditional leaders.

However, as with the other cases of the collective flexing of power that I have discussed, the adoption of a legalistic stance is also available to individual cooperative members. In the nineteenth century, this counterlegalism was used successfully by individual ex-members of utopian-communist religious societies to sue for the right to reclaim their investment from the collective (Weisbrod 1980).

Philosophy of sanctioning

Sanctioning in collective structures is designed to bring the individual to accept responsibility for his own behavior by reminding him of his connectedness to other members of the collective. The major sanctions used are collective persuasion through approval or disapproval, expressed through public opinion, personal appeals, withdrawal of cooperation, ostracism, shaming, and expulsion. The general philosophy behind each of these controls is to restore the wholeness of social existence to the collective after it has been breached by a person's failure to accept responsibility and connectedness. Informal procedure operates as a continuous control on each member's behavior and one that constitutes 'a censorship of the most irresistible nature,' provided that it is based upon 'the spontaneous decisions of the understanding' (Godwin, cited by Woodcock 1962:83-4).

If this series of informal sanctions fails, collective justice can get very rough. Even the relatively mild ongoing criticism can be an effective inducement to radical self-discipline, as with three members of the electronics commune who in each case had trouble fitting in with the cooperative spirit: 'They were told in the way that the rest of us are always criticizing each other. This hurt their pride too much, and they left.' More chillingly, in a housing cooperative, people had just had enough of one or two members who were trying to gain personal power: 'They were obnoxious sort of dominant figures and people decided to give them the boot by no other way than making them feel unwelcome at committee meetings.'

In short, collective persuasion can either work to correct the individual's behavior, such that the connections are reestablished positively, or else it can lead to the member deciding that s/he does not want to take that responsibility, in which case s/he may voluntarily leave the cooperative. As Godwin again astutely observes, 'Under the unequivocal disapprobation and observant eye of public judgement' they are 'inevitably obliged... either to reform or emigrate' (Godwin 1946:211, 340).

However, it is not always an individual alone who takes responsibility for breaking the cooperative spirit of responsibility and connectedness to others. The other members also share this responsibility. Wieck (1978:234) recognizes this when he says 'reparation would not always be exclusively a demand made on a guilty person, but a task for the community concurrently.' Indeed, I have described the approach as *celebrative* (Henry 1983:94-5, 179-219) to reflect the view that deviance, rather than necessarily being seen as a negative experience, may sometimes, and ideally often, contribute positively toward the cooperative's need to revise its relationships in order to adapt to changing circumstances. In this view, deviant behavior may be no more than an indicator of new direction and the deviant a kind of Durkheimian functional rebel (Durkheim 1953).

Melville (1972:130) has pointed out that where there is no general agreement about a problematic behavior, it is 'a sign that part of the group should leave and form another community.' Indeed, a member of a housing cooperative told me that their problem of non-participation was reduced not by conventional discipline, but by restructuring; instead of the individual being forced to fit the group, the group changed to fit the individual.

> As the coop grew, many members began to feel less a part of it... We made the decision to break down into area groups for each group to have its own meeting and control over its own affairs. As a result there has been much more interest shown by the members in the coop's affairs and some of those who had lost interest began to get involved again.

This is a process Taylor (1982:92) describes as fissioning, one that he says may occur 'when there is persistent internal conflict.' As a member of a computer cooperative said, 'I think, in a sense, that's why we only vaguely talk about strategies for discipline, because the ideal solution is to split.'

In short, then, under the collective model of discipline, the sanctioning philosophy is often one of turning negative connectedness into positive by reminding individuals of their responsibilities. It is a celebration of human agency over negative structures that necessarily involves 'acts of imagination... to rectify injustice, to resolve conflict, just as acts of imagination are called for in the normal creation of ongoing life' (Wieck 1978:235).

Interpenetration and contamination: cooperative justice as a semiautonomous field

A crucial issue for cooperatives is whether contradictions such as those discussed above are inherent in any collective system of justice, or whether they occur primarily as a result of the cooperative being contaminated by the wider capitalist structure in which it is set. Some analytical help is available from Moore's concept of semiautonomous fields that she developed to explain her idea of law as process. She starts out arguing that;

> any analysis which focuses entirely on the orderly and the rule bound is limited indeed, and does not place the normative in the context of the whole context of action, which certainly includes much more than conformity to or deviance from normative rules (Moore 1978:3).

She says that instead, 'one is dealing with *partial* order and *partial* control and a central concern must be to identify those social processes which operate outside of the rules, or which cause people to use the rules or abandon them, bend them, reinterpret them, side-step them, or replace them' (Moore 1978:4). Of course, established rules exist, but for Moore these operate in the context of changing moments of time, shifting persons, altering situations, improvised actions, indeterminacy, ambiguity, uncertainty and manipulability:

> Order never fully takes over, nor could it. The cultural, contractual and technical imperatives always leave gaps, require adjustments and interpenetrations to be applicable to particular situations, and are themselves full of ambiguities, inconsistencies and often contradictions (Moore 1978:39).

From this perspective, then, law and social order is an active process, 'not something which once achieved, is fixed.'

Rather, 'existing orders are endlessly vulnerable to being unmade, remade, and transformed, and that even maintaining and reproducing themselves, staying as they are, should be seen as a process' (Moore 1978:6). In order to analyze 'law as process,' Moore (1978:55-6) proposed the concept of the semiautonomous field that can 'generate rules and customs and symbols internally,' and has 'rule-making capacities and the means to induce or coerce compliance.' At the same time, however, the semiautonomous field is 'vulnerable to rules and decisions and other forces emanating from the larger world by which it is surrounded.' She argues that it is 'set in a larger social matrix which can and does invade it.'

Clearly, Moore's semiautonomous field applies to our discussion of the rule making and enforcement practices that form the collective law of cooperatives in capitalist society. We have seen, for example, how cooperatives, while having their own rules and procedures, are also invaded from the wider capitalist society by specialization, hierarchicalization, legalism, sexism, and materialism. Indeed, to some extent, the attribution of invasion is made by cooperative members themselves: 'Specialization,' said a member of the theatre coop, 'is exactly the sort of contradiction that happens when you try and behave in a way that is contradicted by life, by the particular form of our society. You can't avoid it.' Hierarchy, as a member of a housing cooperative pointed out, is difficult for people to avoid. If they expect a landlord-tenant relationship, they cannot imagine how Joe and Mabel from up the road can actually evict them. Nor can Joe or Mabel see themselves evicting someone: 'It's a question of people having been traditionally in a very weak position, and suddenly, they are in a position of power, but are not aware of it, cannot comprehend it.' Sexist divisions are perhaps the most pervasive insofar as their invasion often remains implicit, as we saw earlier.

Others, such as a member of a wholefood cooperative, displayed how existing in a capitalist structure meant materialist interaction for economic survival:

I see a lot of cooperatives very concerned with the superficial image of whether or not they are a kind of far out place. No profit, no authority structure, everybody just does their own thing. Profit means having a surplus at the end of the year rather than a deficit. If you keep having a deficit you go bankrupt.

For a member of the theatre cooperative such contamination was accepted as inevitable:

> No more do I believe we operate perfectly as a collective could operate. Obviously, it's contradicted by lots of things in the outside world. We are on one level a cooperative experimenting with new ways of doing things, and on another we are a small company concerned with developing plays. One thing beyond anything else that makes that possible is economic survival. If you want to eat and do community theatre, it's necessary to earn money, and that means endless concessions.

In short, the tendency for cooperatives to assimilate organizational features directly contradictory to their egalitarian collectivist aims can be seen to stem from the cooperative's semiautonomous nature as a field of rule making set in the wider matrix of capitalism. Moreover, as we saw in the case of housing cooperatives that resorted to the capitalist rational legal control to discipline their uncooperative members, invasion is often invoked by members in their collective attempt to solve recurring problems. These problems themselves are rooted in the outside structure and the ambivalent relations that its members have with people in that structure. The difficulty is well captured by Rothschild-Whitt (1979:522) who says: 'It is asking in effect that people in collectivist organizations constantly shift gears, that they learn to act one way inside their organizations and another outside.'

As we have seen throughout this chapter, if a collective acknowledges the existence of the outside structure in its own internal relations, regardless of whether this is in support or opposition, this can be drawn on as a resource and turned back on the collective, undermining its survival and sapping its spirit. It is for this reason that cooperatives are so vulnerable to individual members. And this, in turn, is the pathway whereby capitalist society is invited to invade to the point of rendering the collective unstable.

In a series of stimulating papers, Fitzpatrick (1983a, 1983b, 1984) develops Moore's notion of semiautonomous fields into what he describes as a theory of 'integral plurality,' whose full ramifications for non-state forms of social control I have explored elsewhere (Henry 1985, 1987a, 1987b). For the present discussion, it will suffice to summarize Fitzpatrick's

(1984:115) central argument, that the wider system of 'state law is integrally constituted in relation to a plurality of social forms.' What this means is that wider structural elements, such as law, economic relations, education, etc., shape semiautonomous fields through a dialectical process of convergence, or coalescence and divergence, or separation. The result is that law transforms the forms with which it is interrelated, in our case cooperative justice, into its own image and likeness. This transformation is not complete, however, since cooperatives, like other social forms with which the wider structure is interrelated, are partially autonomous, retaining some of their own identity in the process. Moreover, as Fitzpatrick argues, the interrelationship is such that the invasion is also two way; in its resistance to total transformation, local social forms are in effect invading the wider structure. In our example, law itself is transformed insofar as it accepts and adjusts to the existence of the cooperatives' collective justice.

Unfortunately, much of Fitzpatrick's argument demonstrates the overarching power of the wider structure to penetrate the local form. This is especially likely in the case of an egalitarian collective, since not many of these exist. Consequently, the number of contacts and opportunities for transforming the wider totality are insignificant relative to those where the collective can be invaded by the wider structure or its representative social forms. (See Henry 1985 for an elaboration of these arguments).

In contrast to much materialist theorizing, however, Fitzpatrick, like Moore, is very aware that the wider structure of society is not wholly determining. He argues that while the law of the state might have overall control, it allows, and to a considerable extent relies upon, the internal autonomy of the local forms with which it is in relation:

> Law sets and maintains an autonomy for opposing social forms keeping them apart from itself and purporting to exercise an overall control, but this control is merely occasional and marginal... In this limited nature of its involvement with other social forms, law accepts the integrity of that which it 'controls.' Its penetration is bounded by the integrity of the opposing social form (Fitzpatrick 1984:126).

Perhaps even more disturbing for cooperatives seeking collectively to establish rules and order is Fitzpatrick's observation that the wider structure can actually gain support via this distancing, and that it often is enhanced the more it is opposed. This is more than the simple expression of the functions of conflict; rather, it is an elaboration of the contradictory tension of dialectical relationships. For example, the housing cooperative's visits system for collecting rent arrears, discussed earlier, allowed a subcommittee of the collective to privately police cooperative members to the point of harassment, intimidation, and victimization. While capitalist law always is able to intervene, this does not occur often in such cases since, just like domestic family disputes or industrial conflict, the matter is seen as a private one between the parties concerned.

Moreover, allowing the visits system to be played out by the cooperative actually serves to strengthen members' respect for the wider system of capitalism. It reinforces, for both the visitors and the visited, the capitalist view of credit and debt, but it also demonstrates the value of capitalist legality's impersonal, rational, and predictable procedures. As the housing cooperative member explained when justifying the cooperative's introduction of a new rational, legally enforced, rent system:

> A system where you don't have to go and explain why you haven't paid and don't have to involve yourself in totally irrelevant personal problems, has to be preferable. So that's why we introduced the new system... if there's a good rent system I don't see why anybody should be intimidated, humiliated.

In short, allowing oppositional structures can actually generate support for the wider structure of capitalism and simultaneously infuse aspects of capitalism into the collective system.

It is for this reason that when collective structures are established within a wider capitalist societal system that has its own history and practice, they are inevitably unstable. Since the only medium available for generating new collective forms is that tied to and constitutive of the wider capitalist structure, then attempts to break away from that structure are often confounded. Marx (1852:115) recognized the duality facing practitioners of radical change in his observation that:

> The tradition of countless dead generations is an incubus to the mind of the living. At the very times when they seem to be engaged in revolutionizing themselves and their circumstances, in creating

something previously non-existent, at just such epochs of revolutionary crisis they anxiously summon up the spirits of the past to their aid, borrowing from them names, rallying cries, costumes, in order to stage the new world historical drama in this time-honored disguise and borrowed speech.

For Marx, the crucial issue for revolutionary change was whether the concepts of the past could be used selectively to enable the liberation of the future. Until the spirit of revolutionary change could be captured and used without reference to the past, automatically and spontaneously, it was but a bourgeois revolution, short-lived, soon reaching its climax.

So it is with cooperatives under capitalism. While the basic idea of cooperatives will emerge in response to the contradictions of capitalism, beyond that, invasion by the wider system is likely whenever new problems arise. This is because the readily available resources for addressing these problems are those generated, tried, and tested as answers to problems of capitalist development. Because of its emergent nature, the collective structure has a limited set of solutions available. The result is that situations requiring new formulations are often answered with old recipes, as in the case of the use of law to back up the housing cooperative's problem of rent arrears. While this may have the effect of temporarily resolving the cooperative's immediate crisis, it simultaneously remakes the old structure and undermines the necessary elaboration of that which is emergent. Until cooperatives can resist the temptation to embrace the apparent security of the past, until they can disinvest in unwittingly constructing that which is, they will be unable to gain a permanent release from their self-generated subordination.[2]

Notes

[1] This analysis draws largely on data that I collected in the course of a wider study on non-state forms of social control (Henry 1983). The research entailed tape-recorded, unstructured interviews with twenty-seven members of twelve different housing, worker, and consumer cooperatives; correspondence with eighty-one housing cooperatives and twenty worker cooperatives; and attending nineteen meetings of one housing cooperative over a four month period. The data were gathered in England in 1979 and 1980. The research was funded by the British Economic and Social Research Council grant no. HR5907/2 while I was a Research Fellow at Middlesex Polytechnic's Centre for Occupational and Community Research.

[2] For an elaboration of these ideas see Henry 1987b. Here I formulate the concept of 'replacement discourse' to capture the essence of a reflexive communication, whereby members of a cooperative might transcend their tie to the existing dominant structure by investing in alternative forms while simultaneously ceasing to invest in existing ones.

Bibliography

Abel, R. 1982. 'A Socialist Approach to Risk.' In *Maryland Law Review*, 41:695-754.

Durkheim, E. 1953. *Sociology and Philosophy.* New York: Free Press.

Ehrlich, E. 1913. *Fundamental Principles of the Sociology of Law.* Cambridge, Mass: Harvard University Press.

Fitzpatrick, P. 1983a. 'Law, Plurality and Underdevelopment.' In *Legality, Ideology and the State* (ed) D. Sugarman. London: Academic Press.

Fitzpatrick, P. 1983b. 'Marxism and Legal Pluralism.' In *Australian Journal of Law and Society*, 1:45-59.

Fitzpatrick, P. 1984. 'Law and Societies.' In *Osgood Hall Law Journal*, 22:115-38.

Gaus, G. and Chapman, J. 1978. 'Anarchism and Political Philosophy: An Introduction.' In *Anarchism* (eds) J.R. Pennock and J.W. Chapman. New York: New York University Press.

Geras, N. 1983. *Marx and Human Nature: Refutation of a Legend.* London: New Left Books.

Godwin, W. 1946. *Political Justice.* Toronto: University of Toronto Press.

Gurvitch, Georges 1947. *Sociology of Law.* London: Routledge and Kegan Paul.

Henry, S. 1983. *Private Justice: Towards Integrated Theorizing in the Sociology of Law.* London: Routledge and Kegan Paul.

Henry, S. 1985. 'Community Justice, Capitalist Society and Human Agency: The Dialectics of Collective Law in the Cooperative.' In *Law and Society Review*, 19:301-25.

Henry, S. 1987a. 'Private Justice and the Policing of Labor: The Dialectics of Industrial Discipline.' In *Private Policing* (eds) C. Shearing and P. Stenning. Beverley Hills: Sage Publications.

Henry, S. 1987b. 'The Construction and Deconstruction of Social Control: Thoughts on the Discursive Production of State Law and Private Justice.' In *Transcarceration: Essays in the Sociology of Social Control* (eds) J. Lowman, R. Menzies and T. Palys. London: Gower press.

King, M. 1981. *The Framework of Criminal Justice*. London: Croom Helm.

Marx, K. 1852. 'The Eighteenth Brumaire of Louis Bonaparte.' In K. Marx and F. Engels *Werke* in *The Portable Marx* (ed) E. Kamenka. Harmondsworth: Penguin, 1984.

Melville, K. 1972. *Communes in the Counterculture*. New York: William Mason.

Moore, S.F. 1978. *Law as Process*. London: Routledge and Kegan Paul.

Olson, M. 1965. *The Logic of Collective Action*. Cambridge, Mass: Harvard University Press.

Proudhon, P. 1876. *What is Property? An Inquiry into the Principle of Right and Government*. New York: H. Fertig.

Ritter, A. 1978. 'The Anarchist Justification of Authority.' In *Anarchism* (eds) J.R. Pennock and J.W. Chapman. New York: New York University Press.

Ritter, A. 1980. *Anarchism, A Theoretical Analysis*. Cambridge: Cambridge University Press.

Rosner, M. 1973. 'Direct Democracy in the Kibbutz.' In *Communes: Creating and Managing the Collective Life* (ed) R. Kanter. New York: Harper.

Rothschild-Whitt, J. 1979. 'The Collectivist Organization: An Alternative to Rational Bureaucratic Models.' In *American Sociological Review*, 44:509-27.

Schwartz, R. 1954. 'Social Factors in the Development of Legal Control: A Case of Two Israeli Settlements.' In *ale Law Journal*, 63:471.

Schwartz, R. 1957. 'Democracy and Collectivism in the Kibbutz.' *Social Problems*, 5:137-47.

Shapiro, A. 1976. 'Law in the Kibbutz: A Reappraisal.' In *Law and Society Review*, 10:415-38.

Taylor, M. 1982. *Community, Anarchy and Liberty.* Cambridge: University Press.

Unger, R. 1975. *Knowledge and Politics.* New York: Free Press.

Unger, R. 1976. *Law in Modern Society.* New York: Free Press.

Weisbrod, C. 1980. *The Boundaries of Utopia.* New York: Pantheon.

Wieck, D. 1978. 'Anarchist Justice.' In *Anarchism* (eds) J.R. Pennock and J.W. Chapman. New York: New York University Press.

Woodcock, G. 1977. *The Anarchist Reader.* London: Fontana.

Woodcock, G. 1962. *Anarchism: A History of Libertarian Ideas and Movements.* New York: The World Publishing Company.

Young, J. 1981. 'Thinking Seriously About Crime: Some Models of Criminology.' In *Crime and Society* (ed) M. Fitzgerald. London: Routledge and Kegan Paul.

5 Hidden hierarchies in Israeli kibbutzim[1]

GERALD MARS

ABSTRACT

Kibbutzim have surprised observers in that they not only have survived, but flourished, while retaining explicit values of economic and social equality. A closer study of kibbutzim, however, reveals how tensions between economic efficiency and egalitarian values have resulted in the emergence of rules that permit economic and social inequality in ways that do not appear to violate egalitarian principles in the eyes of participants or outsiders who share the explicit value system.

It is now close to a century since the first of Israel's famed agricultural collectives, the kibbutzim, were established, and 40 years since the last big wave was created after the 1948 war. Despite variations between the two main organizational federations of kibbutzim and their assertions of differences in ideology and practices, they share a common basic structure and have evolved in similar ways. Both federations have flourished and proliferated so that there are close to 270 kibbutzim extant in Israel today. Sufficient time has passed since the founding of the movement for kibbutzim to be assessed against the egalitarian criteria by which they were established and to chart how they have adapted to the massive changes they have faced.

From their beginnings, the kibbutzim were imbued with both socialist and Zionist aspirations (Vital 1975). Both derived from the political ideologies that were a feature of Jewish life in Eastern Europe during the late nineteenth century (Avineri 1981). It was a duality that set apart forerunners of some of the early kibbutzim from the followers of the Bund movement who, though socialist and culturally nationalist, did not share the political nationalism of the kibbutzniks. The vast majority of kibbutzniks, however, always have seen themselves as builders of the nation state, with social obligations extending beyond their kibbutz boundaries.

Accordingly, kibbutzniks have been involved, especially since the establishment of the State of Israel in 1948, not only in helping to run their own kibbutz, but in helping to develop national institutions such as the General Federation of Labour (the Histradut), the Labour Party (Mapai), and the country's second largest bank, Bank Hapoalim (the Workers' Bank). These external obligations, as we shall see, have had important repercussions on the internal working of the kibbutzim. But, it is for their egalitarianism within enclosed settlements and the means adopted to ensure its institutionalization, that kibbutzim have been most celebrated. Their success in achieving these ends will be assessed here.

The kibbutzim had planned that all exploitation of labour should cease; that each should contribute according to his means and each receive according to his need. To achieve these aims, the prime concern has been to institutionalize direct democracy by dispersing authority. This dispersal of authority has been pursued through two main organizational rules.

The first rule establishes the centrality of the kibbutz General Assembly. All major policy decisions affecting the allocation of resources and the application of formal social controls against member deviancy are taken at weekly meetings of the General Assembly that consists of the whole kibbutz membership. It was planned that minor and routine concerns could be delegated to subcommittees, but that the General Assembly should be the ultimate source of all authority. Accordingly, the explicit rule is that the decisions of the General Assembly should take precedence over the decisions of all subcommittees.

The second rule requires the rotation of all managerial tasks in the various kibbutz enterprises and of roles in the internal committee structure. The usual period in office was designed to range from two to three years, but this term has steadily increased.

These rules were designed to prevent the emergence of an established leadership and proletariat. Historically, various auxiliary rules were employed to support the core means to these ends. It was planned to reduce the significance of kinship links and of kin groups by placing a minimum value on marriage (many early kibbutzim for a time abolished all marriage ceremonies); by rules of communal child rearing and communal eating, as well as by rules opening all tasks to either sex. By these means the kibbutz aimed to replace individual nuclear families, with their dispersed and local loyalties, by one overall kibbutz family that would possess a single collective loyalty. Although the core rules persist, at least in some degree, within most kibbutzim, the auxiliary rules all have been heavily eroded. Nuclear, even extended, families have re-emerged, as have gender distinctions in jobs. Tasks such as food preparation and child rearing are now predominantly carried out by women.

Since the kibbutzim were established, they have undergone many changes. These have been dramatic in their impact and especially so during the past twenty years. From being, for the most part, isolated and struggling agricultural units, the kibbutzim have experienced an industrial revolution. They have become capital intensive, sophisticated, and highly successful agribusinesses. Most also have expanded into manufacturing, often of high-technology goods, and many now provide skilled services. For example, several operate in the hotel industry. Kibbutzim have emerged as an essential component of the Israeli economy, are now integrated into world markets, and are seen as the spearhead of efficient innovation. Many of their members now occupy leading positions in the diplomatic service, banking, political life, and the army. They have, in short, seen many of their Zionist aspirations achieved.

These developments raise a number of important questions about the aim of the kibbutzim to institutionalize direct democracy. Have they succeeded in dispersing authority and power? Have they avoided differences in wealth? The established wisdom of social science would indicate that the cards are strongly stacked against the kibbutzim maintaining their egalitarian structure. It is generally held that voluntary organizations founded on egalitarian principles can survive only by undergoing transformation into hierarchical systems. This position was articulated clearly in the sociology of religion by Max Weber (1921) as *routinization*; the gradual transformation from sect to denomination. Robert Michels (1915) described the same process as the *iron law of oligarchy* or the emergence of the customary right to office.

Contrary to this dominant theoretical tradition, most scholars of kibbutzim seem to agree with Rosner and Cohen (1980) that they have successfully resisted Michels' iron law. Rosner and Cohen write that:

> ... in spite of the basic changes undergone by most of the kibbutzim in the last 15 to 20 years, no basic transformation of the organizational structure has taken place and the description of the principles of this structure as opposed to the bureaucratic ideal type is still accurate for most of them.

This view is supported by Yuchtman-Yaar (1983) in an influential review of the field, wherein he writes:

> The kibbutz movement has apparently been successful in countervailing many of the detrimental conse- quences (of industrialization) by reliance on a series of organizational principles - the most important of which are direct democracy and managerial rotation....

The question arises of whether the kibbutzim really have succeeded in circumventing the development of the customary right to office through the rule of managerial rotation. If they have not, what is it about the way kibbutzim operate their explicitly egalitarian rules that permits the growth of inequality, whilst concealing it from kibbutzniks and observers alike?

To examine these issues requires consideration of whether and, if so, how far the kibbutzim's organizational structures have been transformed during the past twenty years. On this basis, it will be possible to assess whether the core rules on which these structures were established are indeed still operative.

A limited pilot study of three kibbutzim, sustained by numerous interviews with the members and officials of various others, yields two tasks for this paper. First is to demon- strate how and why the kibbutzim have fundamentally adapted

101

the rules by which their organizational structures operate. Second is to explain not only how these changes have occurred, but how and why the most significant of these adaptations, leading to the negation of direct democracy, remain hidden by the same rules system from both the kibbutzniks themselves and systematic observers like Rosner and Cohen.

It would appear that the commentators have seen what the kibbutzniks themselves see, only a part of the reality. The kibbutz rules system is like an iceberg; much of it is invisible, and this invisibility involves the operation of rules that conceal the erosion of direct democracy and the development of a kibbutz elite and proletariat.

Observers of small-scale collective organizations often have argued that scale is the main variable on which the ideal of direct democracy is likely to founder (Taylor 1982). Their claim is that an increase in scale generates an associated division of labour. The division of labour is linked to the formation of an elite that comes to control information that, in turn, ensures its monopoly of power. Examining the kibbutzim from this standpoint, we find all of these characteristics, but not associated with any increase in scale. Although we find increased division of labour, the formation of an elite controlling information, and a resultant monopoly of power, these developments have not arisen as a result of growth in the size of kibbutzim. Most still number no more than 350-500 members, barely exceeding the target sizes achieved shortly after they first were established.

We, therefore, have to look to explanations other than increasing scale for these developments. Part, but only part, of the answer is to be found in the organizational effects flowing from the industrial revolution that has overtaken kibbutzim during the past quarter century. Most have adopted sophisticated technology, both to replace the simpler tasks of agriculture and to form the bases of their industries. Accordingly, a developed division of labour has emerged to operate this technology. As is the case elsewhere, new roles for technocrats and organizational specialists have emerged.

The old organizational duo of Secretary (Maskier) and Treasurer (Gisbar) have found their tasks inordinately more complicated than before, often with a resultant need to supervise and coordinate the work of several assistants. Their roles frequently have been supplemented by a specialist Coordinator of Economic Affairs (Merakes), who acts as overall strategic planner. As the range of kibbutz enterprises expands, an additional range of new and often very powerful officeholders, such as hotel and factory managers, emerges to add to what is, in fact, a new and growing elite.

The knowledge these people need to perform their work is often complex, sometimes highly specialized, and its value is always enhanced by experience. As a result, their replacement through the rotation of managerial tasks, a feature of the agricultural phase of kibbutz development, is now no longer appropriate or, in many cases, even feasible. The kibbutzim have responded by retaining the principle of rotation cosmetically adapted to retain the personal links between scarce expertise and the performance of specific roles.

One way of reconciling the principle of rotation with the personal acquisition of expertise is to allow formal rotation to occur, but only within limited fields; for example, the kibbutz secretary alternating his job with his deputy, and vice versa. Another allows for what often turns out to be regular extensions of office for what are stated to be temporary periods or for the duration of a particular crisis.

A third strategy permits periodic rotation downward in status terms to a publicly visible change of role. The successful administrator, kibbutz secretary, coordinator, or treasurer, is taken from his post and, in effect, put on display in a demonstrably low-status post that is fully visible to the whole kibbutz. Most commonly, the post is that of food server or table cleaner in the communal dining room or some similar task, such as dishwasher, that is not highly regarded, but is in the public eye. Such a change in role, however, rarely extends much beyond a three-month period.

Hence, according to Rayner's principle of mutual substitutability of roles (this volume), all of these strategies disqualify the kibbutz as a strictly egalitarian system. Even the strategy of temporary role change is rather a symbolic assertion of abstract moral equality rather than a practical rotation of responsibilities (a dishwasher is unlikely to be allocated the responsibilities of kibbutz secretary).

The kibbutzim have developed rules that symbolically preserve the equality embodied in the principle of rotation while negating the principle of strict equality that it was originally intended to uphold. This alteration in the application of the rule of job rotation clears the way for the consolidation of an emerging elite.

Other developments have supported the formation of both an

elite and a proletariat that remain largely invisible to both participants and observers of the kibbutzim. As organization within the kibbutz has become more complex, there has developed simultaneously a need for more transactions across the boundary between the community and the outside world. With a simple agrarian technology, little division of labour, and considerable self-sufficiency, the kibbutzim traditionally had maintained a degree of boundary closure. As these traditional features of the kibbutz have eroded, kibbutz functionaries have been increasingly drawn beyond the boundary. They have had to negotiate with more sellers of raw materials, more buyers of their final products, larger numbers of government officials, and many sources of finance.[2] In the process, they require access to resources beyond the reach of the ordinary kibbutz member. They need personal transport, expense accounts, travel abroad, and greater control over their time, much of which might well be spent out of the kibbutz.

Access to special resources separates the kibbutz elite in lifestyle and world view from the people they represent. They not only become involved in a variety of reference groups external to the kibbutz, but develop multiple loyalties and sometimes have to conclude deals involving payoffs that would not always be seen as in the short-term interest of their kibbutz. In carrying out these external activities, members of the kibbutz elite are drawn increasingly apart from their constituents. At the same time, the elite obtain access to information not available to ordinary members, and thus, are able to limit the choices and discretion open to other kibbutzniks. As Rayner (1986) argues of other egalitarian voluntary groups, control over the boundary, rather than mere customary right to office, is the key to the emergence of the kibbutz elite.

As a result of these developments, the relative power of the elite has increased while that of ordinary members has declined. Accordingly, the power of the General Assembly, whose members lack the specialist knowledge and information necessary to make informed decisions on increasingly complex matters, also has declined (Ben-Rafael et al 1973). The power of its subcommittees, dominated by experts and administrators, has increased correspondingly.

It has been observed that strongly bounded egalitarian groups are particularly vulnerable to instability and fission (Douglas 1978). Lacking a hierarchy, they find difficulties in maintaining internal coherence, largely because they possess no ready means for resolving disputes. They characteristically cohere by focusing attention upon their boundaries, that is, by maintaining a strict distinction between outsiders and insiders, emphasizing the evils of external hierarchies in contrast to the moral superiority of their own internal egalitarianism. Traversing the boundary, therefore, is a dangerous task; those who do it are invariably liable to perceived moral contamination and to scapegoating.

Comparative experience, therefore, would lead one to expect the kibbutz air to be thick with accusations against elite members. Indeed, one would expect them to have been picked off, one by one, well before they could consolidate and emerge as a group. Why has this not occurred?

At least part of the explanation is that as the kibbutzim have matured, key administrative positions have tended to be taken by pioneers. Thus, support groups have coalesced around age and similarity of experience (the pioneers versus the newcomers); around kinship (the pioneers and their extended families versus the newer entrants), and around the possession of specialized skills (the organizers and meritocrats, who are heavily drawn from pioneers, versus the rest). These divisions have all served to encourage the consolidation of elites drawn from the pioneers whose overall interests have fused around the need for effective managerial teamwork.

It may be true that newcomers are more likely to observe the disparity between the new reality and the egalitarian ideology of the kibbutz that initially attracted them than are the elite's pioneer cohorts who gradually absorbed changes in the operation over the years, though not the explicit principle of the rotation rule. However, it would be much harder for newcomers to muster support against the pioneer elite than for the pioneers to arrange the exclusion of newcomers as 'not kibbutz material.'

A further explanation of why the kibbutzim have refrained from internal witch hunting and have overlooked the emergence of hierarchy lies in the persistent crises that have faced the State of Israel since its foundation in 1948. The egalitarian groups' cultural metaphor of the wall of virtue protecting members from enemies without is particularly poignant in the State of Israel, and appears to have contributed to the consolidation of kibbutz elites. Rayner (1982), discussing the geographical and spatial perceptions of egalitarian sects, describes their recursive patterning of spatial boundaries, discriminating increasing levels of threat beyond the borders of the group. Along the same lines, a threat to Israel is readily translatable into a direct threat to the kibbutz itself, promoting solidarity and distracting attention from internal divisions. This is particularly so since many kibbutzim have been strategically sited on the country's borders.

Having an external enemy, often literally at the gate, also has served to emphasize to kibbutzniks their necessary involvement with the pressing concerns of the wider society. The protection of the State of Israel, including the provision of recruits for the armed services and support for the defence system, are legitimate external concerns of kibbutzim in accord with the original Zionist ideal. Hence, boundary crossing for these legitimate purposes may have served to make the elite's activities more acceptable to the ordinary kibbutznik. In this case, the elite would be seen to serve as a buffer between the kibbutz and the outside world, preserving the internal egalitarian order rather than demonstrating the existence of a hierarchy within the kibbutz itself.

Closer examination reveals that the kibbutz has two buffers: one, an elite that traverses the boundary from within; the other, a proletariat that traverses the boundary from without. Rayner (1982), in his study of a strongly bounded Maoist commune, identified a periphery of supporters that was given partial access to the group and its resources in return for acting as a buffer to maintain the commune's separation from mainstream London society. Such an entity of non-member supporters operating between a sect and the outside world appears to be commonplace. These peripheries might well be functionally essential to the continued existence of sects, communes, and collectives. Thus, monastic orders have similarly active peripheries of lay brothers: the Whirling Dervishes of Konya in Turkey have a lay periphery called 'Friends of the Mevlana'; while Jews in the pre-holocaust small settlements of Eastern Europe, called Shtetl (Zborowski and Herzog 1952), had a periphery of gentiles, Shabbes Goyim, so called because they performed special functions for Jews on the Sabbath.

All of these strongly bounded entities use their peripheries in the same way; to mediate between them and the threatening, polluting outside as well as to perform services too contaminating for their own core members.

In each case, periphery members are allowed little or no role in the formation of policies or in the allocation of resources. Their members' prestige, when viewed from within, is lower and their relationships more shifting than are those of the core they serve. Although periphery members, in some cases, may be used as a reservoir for selective recruitment, full members of the collective would never confuse the two entities. Members define both periphery and core as separate and distinct. Their boundaries are too tightly drawn, as they see it, for ambiguity or incorporation.

The periphery differs importantly from the elite buffer in that the elite insulates the group from the pressures of the State or other authority that might claim the allegiance of the membership, while the periphery insulates the group from pressures arising from face-to-face interactions with ordinary members of the wider society.

Just such a periphery is to be found around the vast majority of kibbutzim. It consists of foreign student volunteers who spend periods of a few months to a year working in kibbutz factories and farms in exchange for food, accommodation, pocket money, and the experience of learning about a foreign country. The students constitute a separate kibbutz proletariat, socially distinct from permanent members. They live in separate compounds, and cannot vote in assemblies. Although the constituency continually changes, the number of peripheral members mostly is kept below about 20 percent of the size of the kibbutz permanent membership.

It is in their economic relation to production as manual workers who lack capital that we can identify the entity of students as a proletariat. Their relative lack of power over the allocation of resources and the making of policy, their lower level of prestige in the eyes of core members, and their lower level of economic reward are certainly indicative of a proletariat. But it is their role as labourers who lack capital that crucially defines them as such.

The fact that the permanent members invariably conceive of their social boundaries so tightly that they refuse to acknowledge their systemic connection to the volunteer periphery should not blind us to its proletarian function. By looking beyond the internal definition, by examining the systemic criteria of how the rules actually operate rather than using only the internal ideological criteria of how the kibbutzim see the rules that they apply to themselves, we make visible a new boundary. The systematic refusal to recognize the functionally integrated periphery as true members of the collective permits the kibbutzim to maintain the ideology of equality in the face of increasing specialization and selective extension of privileges.

We can conceptualize the argument as a concealed breakdown of the egalitarian rules of the kibbutz founders in five phases leading to the establishment of both a hidden hierarchy and a hidden proletariat.

The five-phase breakdown of kibbutz egalitarianism

Phase I

Closed boundary; simple division of labour, mostly based on agriculture; visibility of egalitarian rules strictly enforced; rotated tasks; common decision making.

Phase II

An increasing need for cross-boundary transactions, bulk purchases and sales, negotiations with government, raising of finance and the solving of disputes, both within and between kibbutzim.

Phase III

Boundary permeable; increased division of labour. Boundary managers emerge with claims to special resources: transport, travel, expense accounts, personal control of time. They become buffers to external reference groups.

Phase IV

Consolidation of boundary managers controlling information, especially information available only to those crossing boundary. Limits choices and discretion available to other members. Managers interact to become a management team with external orientation.

Phase V

External competition encourages further division of labour and management specialization. Growth of operating proletariat supplied by foreign students.

Summary

The egalitarian group in Phase I has turned into a classic pyramid in Phase V. But the additions of the elite and the proletariat remain invisible to the permanent inhabitants of the kibbutz and, it would seem, to external commentators who accept the same internal definition of kibbutz rules of decision making and membership. The elite is invisible because of the cosmetic adaptation of rule by the General Assembly and symbolic job rotation. The proletariat is invisible because the boundary rule separating it from the permanent members is conceptually, though not systemically, exclusive, and because its personnel, being transitory, can develop no collective memory that would assert a re-examination of its situation.

Notes

[1] I thank Steve Rayner for his careful advice in the preparation of this paper. I also have discussed aspects of the paper at various times with Michel Altman, David Binns, Mary Douglas, Gidean Kressel, and Len Mars. Their comments have been most helpful. I am grateful, too, for the generous assistance given me by a variety of Chaverim from different kibbutzim.

[2] Many of these transactions have been found to be better served when negotiators can act for several kibbutzim. This cooperation has led to sources of power developing outside the kibbutz, located in the federations. After a series of amalgamations, there are now two main federated groupings. They are staffed by delegates from the constituent kibbutzim, and their posts are rotated in the same way as are kibbutz posts.

Bibliography

Avineri, S. 1981. *The Making of Modern Zionism*. London: Weidenfeld and Nicholson.

Ben-Rafael, E., Livneh and Wolfensohn 1973. 'Democracy in the Kibbutz.' In *Social Res. Review*, No. 2, Haifa (Heb).

Douglas, Mary 1978. *Cultural Bias*. Occasional Paper 35, Royal Anthropological Institute, London.

Michels, R. 1915. *Political Parties: A Sociological Study of the Oligarchical Tendencies of Modern Democracy*. Glencoe: Free Press.

Rayner, Steve 1982. 'The Perception of Time and Space in Egalitarian Sects: A Millenarian Cosmology.' In *Essays in the Sociology of Perception* (ed) Mary Douglas. London: Routledge & Kegan Paul.

Rayner, Steve 1986. 'The Politics of Schism.' In *Power, Action, and Belief: The New Sociology of Knowledge* (ed) John Law. London: Routledge & Kegan Paul.

Rosner, M. and N. Cohen 1980. 'Is Direct Democracy Feasible in Modern Society?' In *Problems of Integrated Cooperatives in the Industrial Society: The Example of the Kibbutz* (eds) K. Bartolke, Th. Bergman, and L. Liegle. Assen, The Netherlands: Van Gorcum Publishing Co.

Taylor, M. 1982. *Community, Anarchy and Liberty*. Cambridge: Cambridge University Press.

Vital, D. 1975. *The Origins of Zionism*. Oxford University Press.

Weber, M. 1921. *Wirtschaft und Gesellschaft I*. Tubingen, J.C.B. Mohr. *The Theory of Social and Economic Organisation*, 1947. Trans. by A.M. Henderson and Talcott Parsons. New York: MacMillan Press.

Yuchtman-Yaar, E. 1983. 'The Tension Between Communal Values and Economic Imperatives in the Modern Kibbutz.' In *Contempory Sociology*, September.

Zborowski, M. and E. Herzog 1952. *Life is with People: The Culture of the Shtetl*. New York: Schocken Books.

6 Egalitarianism, collectivism and individualism: the Digo of Kenya

LUTHER P. GERLACH AND URSULA M. GERLACH

ABSTRACT

In the late 1950's, all families among the Digo of south coastal Kenya lived at about the same material standard. All adult men appeared able to participate more or less equally in family and community decision making, and women appeared able to prevent men from tyrannizing them. In this sense, the Digo were relatively egalitarian, but not because their social system had yet to evolve the complexities of hierarchy and stratification. They knew about inequality from their association with the Arabs and British as well as from their past, during which their ancestors had been either slave or master to each other, or both, and during which they often had been led by strong men. Digo egalitarianism was a by-product of Digo efforts to escape this past and to negotiate compromises between individual and collective interest. They pressured each other to exchange material wealth for social support, and sought to prevent each other from exercising this social strength to control interpersonal or community decision making. They achieved these objectives by using and manipulating competing and contradictory cultural models in this system; traditional and Islamic, matrilineal and patrilineal. The high value they placed on protecting personal and family pride was illustrated by their attempts to overcome their

history of slavery while suppressing discussion of it. Thus,
Digo egalitarianism was a system of premises, rules, and
processes of considerable complexity.

Introduction

In the introduction to their classic anthology, *African Political
Systems*, editors Meyer Fortes and E.E. Evans-Pritchard (1940)
observe that the traditional social systems described by their
various authors fall into two main types. One type consists
of those systems that are centralized in authority, administrative machinery, and judicial institutions; in short, these
societies have a government. Furthermore, in these systems,
cleavages of wealth, privilege, and status correspond to the
distribution of power and authority. The other type of social
system comprises those societies that lack such governmental
institutions, and in which there is no sharp division of status,
rank, or wealth. Scholars frequently have elaborated upon
this simple dichotomy to fit their fieldwork findings or
particular conceptual approaches (Murdock 1959, Mair 1962,
Bohannan 1963, Schneider 1981), but the dichotomy remains
useful and has framed a number of important questions.

One of the questions addresses the way societies manage
affairs without the explicit institutions of formal and hierarchical government. As Middleton and Tait (1958) put it, how
do tribes without rulers rule? It seems to us that the
answers given by scholars to this question indicate that
Rayner (this volume) is correct when he says that egalitarian
organization depends upon rules systems that may be as
complex as those required for hierarchical society. Fortes and
Evans-Pritchard explain that while centralized systems achieve
stable rule by balancing differing parts of their formal
administrative organization, the non-centralized systems
establish equilibrium among competing segments. The latter
seems as complex a process as the former, even in societies
like that of the Nuer in which the segments are rather neat
patrilineal units nested within each other (Evans-Pritchard
1940a). There are, of course, many non-centralized societies
in Africa in which the segments are composed more elabo-
rately. For example, a not uncommon pattern among societies
that once organized chiefly around matrilineal principles is
that they now also incorporate patrilineal ones, sometimes in

balanced harmony (Forde 1950, 1964), but often in tension (Turner 1957).

One such society is that of the Digo of south coastal Kenya who occupy an area roughly parallel with the Indian Ocean coastline, from Mombasa in Kenya, south to Tanga in Tanzania. There are places along this coast where Digo settlements front the ocean, but during the 1950's, most of the land along the shore was officially held by others, chiefly the British Crown, Indians, and Arabs (Warren 1962). The Digo are classified as northeast coastal Bantu speakers and the southernmost of nine linguistically and culturally related peoples once known as the Nyika, and since independence, as the Mijikenda (Midzichenda), or 'nine cities,' (Prins 1952, Murdock 1959, Gerlach 1965, Parkin 1972). The Digo numbered about 115,000 in 1960.

In the early 1950's, the Digo were described as a non-centralized egalitarian society in which traditional matrilineal and newer patrilineal rules were in tension driven by the Digo conversion to the Islam that had been practiced on the coast by generations of Arab settlers (Prins 1952, Murdock 1959, Trimmingham 1962). We conducted research among the Digo from 1958-1960,[1] chiefly to learn about Islamicization and its impacts. At least since the 1930's, British administrators had worried that Islamicization was complicating, and hence confusing, Digo decision making. The Digo, they feared, could not decide whether Islamic patrilineal or traditional matrilineal rules should be applied in cases of marriage, divorce, and above all, inheritance and succession.

In our research, we found that Islam was only one of the sources of Digo cultural elaboration, and that while the result was complex and may have baffled outsiders, it was well understood by the Digo. The Digo incorporated various apparently contradictory rules from different sources in order to give themselves more flexibility in managing change. We hypothesize that Digo egalitarianism in the 1950's was the result of their complex efforts to balance traditional collectivism with individualism composed of personal pride and a growing entrepreneurial spirit.

History

The Digo had moved into Kenya as early as the 17th century, migrating from the presumed homeland of the Mijikenda in

Somalia, south along the Shimba Hills. To protect themselves from enemies, they lived in compact, walled settlements located at strategic places in these hills (Spear 1976). It is probable that the fortified settlements often were commanded by strong men, and that some of these became powerful enough to rule alliances of several clans and settlements. Apparently, the Digo ranked clans according to the order in which they were believed to have founded these fortified settlements, and they ranked lineages according to the birth order of ancestresses.

From the beginning of their habitation in Kenya, the Digo established important relationships with the various Arabs and Afro-Arabs, or Swahili, peoples who lived and worked in coastal towns and plantations (Coupland 1965, New 1971, Spear 1981). The Digo not only became fluent in Swahili as a second language but, through these relationships, they were able to learn about and to adopt elements of Afro-Arab-Islamic culture, including its system of slavery and social stratification (Salim 1976).

By the end of the 19th century, the British took control of the Kenya coast as a protectorate through treaties they made with the Omani Arab Sultans of Zanzibar. British rule was to affect the evolution of Digo egalitarianism by changing patterns of stratification, hierarchy, and land use.

The Pax Britannica soon stopped the slave trade, and, after 1907, the keeping of slaves. This ban affected the Arabs by depriving them of items of commerce and by releasing the work force that ran their plantations. The resulting vacated coastal land was opened to squatters, both former slaves and Digo.

The acquisition of land was only one effect of the end of slavery on the Digo. Some had participated as middlemen in the slave trade; those who were wealthy enough held work slaves and concubines; and far more importantly, the Digo had had a system of keeping household slaves that was not unlike those reported for other east and central Africans (Turner 1957). Household slaves were held by the Digo as pawns for material debt, taken as compensation for blood debt, or given up by families during times of famine or war. Many of these people bore children to Digo masters, and this history of master/slave relationships continued to affect the daily lives of the Digo.

The rise of egalitarianism

By the 1950's, all of these slave statuses were officially ended, and the Digo sought to integrate themselves into one ostensibly equal people. Many Digo could trace descent from slavery, but they suppressed this heritage, not only because the institution was prohibited by the government, but because continued reference to it could tear asunder their society. The Pax Britannica had promoted egalitarianism by enabling the Digo to leave the protection of their fortified, but often hierarchically governed, settlements, to spread out to farm the previously unoccupied forest, river valley, and vacated plantations. Also, British bans on slavery had created a shortage of labor that was widely felt. Plentiful land and water resources made a satisfying life possible, but only if the Digo could maintain their social cohesion.

The existing conditions also were those favorable to the use of swidden technology, or shifting cultivation with long fallow periods (Schneider 1981). The Digo practiced this form of food production, and the system reinforced their egalitarianism, as it does in many societies (Fortes and Evans-Pritchard 1940). The Digo rejected intensification measures encouraged by the British when these measures threatened to raise the spectre of past slavery and engender hierarchy and social stratification.

For example, the Digo associated certain kinds of labor, such as working in paddy fields, with slavery, therefore, they refused British offers to help them intensify rice cultivation. In addition, the Digo worried that if some of their fellows took advantage of British technical assistance to increase rice production, and sought to establish private rights in river valley land as descendents of early settlers, others would contest these claims on similar grounds. This conflict would increase tension between those using matrilineal rules and those using patrilineal rules of tracing descent. It would inevitably force debate over which claimant line was master, and which was slave; and, if some Digo were successful with intensifying production of rice, others would envy them.

Throughout many of the British attempts at production intensification, there was a misunderstanding of Digo priorities. In allocating land, the Digo traditionally were less interested in gaining material wealth than in protecting social harmony and in enhancing supporter networks. Particularly to the older Digo, hard physical labor was a sign of slavery, and prestige did not lie in working hard to produce ever more food or cash crops. It lay in having the necessities of life, in being surrounded by many dependents and supporters, and in having the leisure to manage social life and political affairs.

Characteristics of egalitarianism

Digo economic egalitarianism was most clearly demonstrated in several ways. Digo families or kin groups shared a similar material standard, had about equal access to land for their major subsistence activities, and used the same horticultural technology. Access to resources producing cash crops, chiefly copra from coconuts, was somewhat uneven, but they actively sought to equalize distribution of income from these crops by encouraging their fellows to share in the course of daily living and through elaborate group rituals.

It is recognized that even in societies considered prototypical of simple egalitarianism, there are inequalities based on age, sex, and personal abilities (Trigger 1985, Service 1975), and the Digo were no exception. The Digo accepted that adult males, often in order of seniority of birth within kin groups, would inherit rights to allocate group land for farming and to manage group property, chiefly coconut palms. Women, children, and the very old were considered dependent upon the greater wisdom of these men, but everyone expected to be consulted in decision making and to be treated with respect. The senior men also were expected to possess a sense of duty to use their rights for the honor and benefit of the group. If the men abused their trust, other members of the group questioned their right to leadership by invoking competing rules of inheritance.

It was possible for individuals, usually young men, to go beyond the use of group resources to make money through business or wage labor. However, they could expect to be pressured strongly to share their gains with kin and affines, always being careful not to injure the pride of others or appear to dominate them. In turn, they would seek to legitimate their quest for gain and more private enterprise by manipulating both customary and new, particularly Islamic, cultural models.

Digo men and women were very proud and sensitive to affronts to their dignity. They did not easily accept control by others, they often resented taking orders, even from close and senior kin and affines, and they expected to be coaxed or cajoled into cooperating. In order to protect their individual rights and dignity and to escape control, they manipulated the Digo kinship system by playing matrilineal against patrilineal kin, and by playing kin against affines.

Regardless of the way they treated one another, the Digo were on the lowest rung in the stratified colonial society, with the British on top and the Arabs and Indians in the middle. Thus, colonial society provided the Digo with models of inequality that they ignored as best they could. As previously mentioned, the British also encouraged the Digo to develop their material resources in ways that would have created a favored elite, but the Digo seldom took this development advice for a number of reasons.

Though subordinated to a centralized British colonial administration, the Digo were politically egalitarian. Each location and village community was governed by a council of adult men cautiously directed by one of their number who was appointed chief by the colonial government. The colonial government wanted such chiefs to be docile enough to take colonial orders and strong enough to implement them, while the Digo wanted them to be docile enough to conform to local expectations, but strong enough to stand up to the colonial administration.

In asserting their egalitarianism, the Digo sought to escape their hierarchical and stratified history. They suppressed memory of a time before Pax Britannica when a few Digo had risen to command large confederacies of Digo clans, and had established chiefdoms apparently modeled on coastal Arab sultanates. Most importantly, the Digo sought to overcome a past in which their ancestors had augmented lineages and households by incorporating pawns and slaves. In the 1950's, many Digo could trace or hide descent from such slaves and/or their masters, depending upon how they used traditional matrilineal or Islamic patrilineal principles. Increasingly, they sought to hide this past.

Challenges and changes

In the effort to surmount the most troubling parts of their stratified past, and to adapt to new social and economic opportunities and problems, one of the main concerns of the Digo was to overcome their heritage of slavery without

119

unravelling their social fabric or releasing memories too destructive of their present. In the past, by using slavery innovatively, the Digo sought to solve economic and social problems by expanding networks of supporters and by developing new settlements. In order to circumvent their matrilineal dilemma, the problem of balancing responsibility between the matrilineages of wife and sister, the Digo retained matriliny both as ideal and practice, while also incorporating the advantages of fathers' rights.

In the 1950's, most Digo sought to adapt further. Families attempted to work their way out of slavery by untangling old webs of obligation even as they wove new ones. Individuals responded to new opportunities to enter trade and expand cash-crop production, while fulfilling obligations to both new and old collectivities and maintaining group and individual pride. There were a few Digo who sought to keep some traditional control as master over those descended from their lineage slaves, but the slaves' descendents resisted subordination. Some slaves sought to break from their master lineage completely and to be redeemed by the lineage, clan, or other tribe from which they or their ancestors had been taken. There were others who simply wished to have their group treated as an equal within the various houses of their former master clan, and as affirmation of this equality, to secure rights to coconut groves and to establish their own graveyards or curing shrines. There were a few others who sought more personal gains and freedoms, although usually the personal and group objectives merged.

Digo adaptations and changes included the use of Islamic family law relating to marriage and inheritance in order to obtain material resources while suppressing slave stigma, the use of traditional rituals and Islamic ideas to work out new, more equitable relationships, and the application of Islamicized curing ritual to control entrepreneurs and to reaffirm collective identity.

Islamic marriage and inheritance as a lever

In the Digo Islamic marriage, payment was divided into three parts; *kilemba*, paid to the bride's father to recompense him for his care of her, *makaya*, to repay her mother for her care, and *mahari*, to be paid by the prospective husband to his bride. The last sum was usually kept by the bride's father, and was meant to ensure that she would be cared for in the event of a divorce.

In Digo Islamic marriages, Parkin (1980) identifies *mahari* as a type of dowry, and Spiro (1975) theorizes generally that dowry is a means of negotiating an improvement in the rank of women. Comaroff (1980) feels that the Mijikenda system of prestations summarized by Parkin 'are much too complex to assimilate to the calculus which underlies Spiro's scheme.' In fact, Digo men sought to use *mahari* more as a part of bridewealth than as dowry, though, technically, it is neither. Digo women sometimes challenged this customary distortion of ideal Islamic law in a way that could enhance their status.

Perhaps beginning in the 1950's, Digo women demanded that *mahari* be paid to them directly, in accordance with the letter of the Islamic marriage law. Sometimes the bride asked this, sometimes her mother. For maximum effect, they made this claim before the Arab-Islamic official, the Mudir, when he recorded a new marriage or came to check the record of marriages completed over several years. This was drastic action. It shamed the bride's kin, her new affines, and the community, particularly if done before the Mudir. The bride was warned that she would be on her own if she was divorced. Yet from 1958-1960 in Lungalunga, three women claimed this right and others used it as a threat, putting perhaps 25% of local Islamic marriages into question. The three women did it because they sought to counter a history of treatment by their fathers and fathers' kin that they felt stigmatized them as descendants of slaves of their fathers' ancestors. In two of these cases, the brides were encouraged by their mothers.

One of these mothers reminded her daughter, Miriamu, that because Miriamu's mother's mother had been brought to Lungalunga as a slave to Miriamu's father's matrilineage, Miriamu had no *kuchetuni*, or mother's side, of her own. The *mahari* in Miriamu's own hands would give her mother both the symbol and the substance of independence and security. The women invested the *mahari* by making interest free loans, *rahani*, to owners of coconut palms, using the trees as collateral, then harvesting the nuts and selling the copra until the loan was repaid. By securing rights in palms, they further established their independence. Another bride who claimed *mahari* used it to establish herself in Mombasa as a prostitute, somewhat in the manner described by Gomm (1972). In order to secure a divorce, she used her earnings as a prostitute to return the *kilemba* and *makaya* prestations to her husband, but refused to return *mahari*, citing Islamic law.

Property

Islamic law also helped the Digo overcome slave heritage by providing a new way to establish patrilineal inheritance of property, chiefly coconut palms. Traditionally, both coconut palms and slaves descended matrilineally. Therefore, sons could inherit property, or use it in anticipation of inheritance, only when they were, in effect, also sister's sons; when their mother had been a slave of their father's lineage, or a descendent of such a slave, and, hence, a 'sister' to their father. In the late 1950's in Lungalunga, there were men important to the community who had inherited, or stood to inherit, valuable coconut groves in exactly this way. The fact of their slave ancestry was not openly admitted, but they and many others worried that those descended from their line of masters might always remind them of it. They were obligated to support their former masters' line socially and financially.

By the 1950's, however, the Digo had agreed that men could inherit from their fathers according to Islamic law, if they could show that both father and son were Muslim. One way to show Muslim status was to be married according to Islamic law. Men were persuaded by their sons and wives, particularly wives with a heritage of slavery, to convert *kuhala*, or traditional, Digo marriages into *kiislamu*, or Digo Islamic marriages. While colonial administrators apparently did not understand how slave heritage motivated Digo action, they did endorse this Islamic method of deciding Digo inheritance. The administrators felt that the new system would bring legal certainty to the Digo, who appeared to be confused by the transition between matriliny and patriliny. This legal code would simplify their tasks as magistrates that, as they reported in their records, had been so greatly complicated by Digo property disputes (Anderson 1954). Both the Digo and the administrators conveniently interpreted Islamic law to mean simply that sons inherit at the expense of other Koranic sharers, including daughters. Daughters could expect their brothers to care for them in customary fashion, as a duty of inheriting the family property.

In seeking to restate and codify Digo law for the newly independent Kenya government, Cotran (1969) distinguished between property of the female side and property of the male side. According to Cotran, the property of the male side referred to land planted by fathers with and for their sons; property of the female side was that long established by matrilineages. In making these distinctions, he followed the advice of Digo elders who served in the Kwale District Court, and Digo in the 1950's also made this distinction.

In theory, this distinction neatly solved inheritance problems. When a man died, his matrikin inherited the property that was theirs by right, while his sons and sons' sons inherited the land he had prepared for them. In practice, inheritance was far more complicated, just as the Digo social organization was complicated. Slave descent that combined the 'male side' and 'female side' had simplified matters originally, but subsequent methods of tracing descent increased the possible inheritance combinations. Islam helped legitimate inheritance by sons through slave mothers, thus camouflaging slave ancestry, but it was also used to help sons claim property from their father's matrilineage. The Digo interpreted father's side to mean father's patrikin, matrikin, or a combination of these. If the Digo had been driven by the desire to exclude as many people as possible from sharing the inherited property, they might have decided quickly upon ways to settle inheritance. But most wished to incorporate as many people as possible into their support networks, and the reward for giving support was to share in property. The Digo accepted the trade off. Besides, it was shameful to lose kin through disputes that reminded everyone of slave history.

It was at the end of the funeral ritual that the kinsmen and affines of the deceased gathered to clear up his affairs, to negotiate both inheritance of his rights and succession to his duties. Those who gathered, even very distant relatives, contributed to a general fund to be used to pay funeral expenses and debts of the deceased. Then a circle of closer kin decided how property would be inherited, and how the dependents of the deceased would be supported. Wives were treated both as dependents and property. Often it was decided that a brother of the deceased, usually uterine, would be trustee until the actual heirs, the sons and sisters' sons, were old enough to manage their own affairs. This entire decision process was usually directed by senior kinsmen of the deceased who should be fair and able to reconcile conflicting interests.

Since property claims were uncertain, whoever inherited or managed the property either shared benefits or expected eventually to be challenged by the other potential heirs and dependents of the deceased. If matrikin were the chief heirs but did not help patrikin, the latter used Islam to contest the settlement. If patrikin did not use their portion to help others, they were challenged by matrikin asserting the preeminence of the female side in Digo history and criticizing *kiislamu* as an Arab import. Those who felt cheated could threaten at any time to bring up a family history of slavery that might shame the contesting groups as well as the community.

When the contesting female side and male side could not settle a dispute, it was heard by an assembly of all the community elders in the *ngambi*, recognized by the colonial government as an informal court. *Ngambi* elders knew the contextual complexities of the dispute and usually resolved it by promoting compromise. Whether negotiated by competing parties alone or through the *ngambi*, compromises usually prevented a few individuals from using property to enrich only themselves, and the resulting agreement characteristically increased the number of those in a property-sharing group by amalgamating male side and female side heirs.

The Digo were motivated further to make the *ngambi* work. In the 1950's, if the *ngambi* failed to resolve a dispute, the disputants took the case into the colonial government court system. The Digo, then, either lost control of the decisions in favor of narrow legalistic interpretations, or they were forced to explain their history to strangers, thus revealing their slaver heritage. The history and operation of the *ngambi* reflected and promoted Digo egalitarianism and the Digo method of negotiating compromise by balancing interests.

The *ngambi*

The *ngambi* is an old institution developed from the Digo age system. Traditionally, positions in the *ngambi* were ranked, and membership in the grade of governing elders was acquired by going through secret initiations and paying fees to the initiators; the fees consisting primarily of palm wine, chickens and goats. Since the fees were made available to the elder through the contributions of his kinfolk, the more people he commanded, the more he could pay, and the higher he could rise. By the 1950's, this old system was dead. Digo remembered little of it, except that it was a 'dangerous, pagan, and dirty' custom due to the unpredictable behavior of the elders when they were drinking during initiation. The Digo said it died because they converted to Islam, banned the drinking of palm wine, and called upon elders to behave with dignity. It also died because one function of the system was to organize young men to fight wars, an activity that the British had stopped.

In the *ngambi* of the 1950's, all adult men participated as a public duty and right, and each location or village community had its own *ngambi*. The government-appointed chief presided over the *ngambi* and acted as intermediary between it and the colonial government. For example, it was the chief who encouraged the *ngambi* to implement government economic policy, and it was the chief who helped the *ngambi* formulate requests for assistance to be taken to the government.

In matters of 'native land and custom,' including marriage and inheritance, the *ngambi* was to act essentially as a council of equals. All community men were, in principle, to have an equal voice in decision making; however, in practice in Lungalunga, some men were more forceful than others and consistently seemed to have somewhat more influence. Sometimes, seniors in sibling groups were the most active and influential, but not always. Much variation can be attributed to individual differences, although, it seems likely that the slave ancestry factor affected interpersonal dynamics in complex and usually covert ways. On the one hand, some men of former master status sought subtly to exercise power; on the other hand, most Digo bent in the opposite direction to demonstrate equality.

The significant overt feature of the *ngambi* that the Digo felt enabled them to resolve disputes in matters of 'native law and custom' was that each member of the *ngambi* sat as a relative and supporter of both plaintiff and defendant, and also could sit as a judge rendering decision. Participants could sit with either party because they could trace relationship as kin or affine to each, and they could also sit as judge as a member of the community. They could make decisions as judges that would be acceptable to the disputants, not because they studiously tried to be neutral and objective, but because they actively demonstrated their equal commitment to each of the conflicting parties.

In the course of a typical process, *ngambi* members sat in the caucus of the plaintiff as his kin, and argued his right to compensation for a wrong done him. By also showing that he was not blameless, they urged the plaintiff to be generous and to seek reconciliation. Then, the same members caucused with the defendant, found extenuating circumstances, and argued for a reduced fine. They also criticized the defendant's behavior and warned him to change or lose their support. In time, many or all joined the circle of their fellows sitting as judges. There they deliberated on the arguments of both sides, and also went back and forth between the causes of defendant and plaintiff, carrying messages and negotiating settlement. Only the defendant and plaintiff played solitary roles, and they said little. Others spoke for them and about them, using indirection and humor to avoid direct confrontation.

Finally, all participants in the discussion convened in a large circle as the *ngambi*, reviewed findings, and came to a decision. If a fine was levied, they returned to their caucuses. Sitting as kin of the defendant, they helped him pay the fine; as kin of the plaintiff, all received a portion of payment as compensation. Then, sitting as judges, they received a portion of the fine as a token of respect. Often a part of the fine was used to buy sodas at the local general store, and these drinks, rather than the traditional palm wine and sacrificed chicken or goat, were ceremonially shared by everyone as members of the *ngambi*, including the defendant and plaintiff. It was expected that, when asked, the Indian owner of the shop would contribute to the soda fund to show respect to the *ngambi* that regulated affairs and kept the peace, all of which helped the shop owner do business. If the *ngambi* dealt with cases involving coconut palms, their owner also could expect to contribute to the soda fund, because he marketed the copra from these palms.

The *ngambi* process dramatized Digo efforts to promote equality and collective concern while protecting individual pride; to balance these conflicting interests while muting overt expression of hostility. In spite of their emphasis on muting conflict and promoting compromise, the Digo sometimes did force matters beyond quiet resolution (thus, perhaps, sanctioning compromise). This escalation happened, for example, when a few women demanded direct payment of *mahari*, not only to gain financially, but to erase the stigma of slave ancestry. In other cases that went beyond quiet resolution,

126

the Digo contested this stigma, either directly, by challenging each other's ancestry in genealogical song duels, or less directly, by attempts to reclaim ancestors, to build ancestral curing shrines, to control decision making about marriage, witchcraft cleansing, funerals and burials. By examining such cases, beginning with the latter, it is possible to follow controversies about control that flowed from master/slave relationships.

Disputed inequality: controlling Nguro's burial

The relationships that underlay a major 1950's dispute about the continuing right of masters to bury their slaves were rooted in the history of two Chinarama matrilineages and the slaves Koche and Gao. Niterema and Nidia were freeborn founders of the two main matrilineages of the Chinarama in Lungalunga, both of which were master lineages. Koche, taken as a slave from the Doe tribe in Tanganyika, was brought into the line of Niterema at the generational level of Nichinyama, a free woman and 'sister' of the slave woman. Koche was given as wife to Gao, the son of another slave woman and a free man of the Chinaniterema. To Koche and Gao were born two daughters, Nigao senior and junior, who each bore a son, Nguro and Budzo (Safari), respectively. Saidi Bamvua, a direct descendant of Niterema through a line of free women, including Nichinyama, was, according to tradition, their master. They and their children used land that his ancestors had given to their ancestors to use, and they used coconut palms that their ancestors had planted with the permission of the Chinaniterema. Traditionally, the families of Nigao senior and junior would have given food from their gardens and coconuts from their grove to the Chinaniterema. In return, they would have been assisted by the Chinaniterema. Though they were members of the master lineage, they were subordinate to it, 'its children.'

Saidi was the senior member of the Chinaniterema line through Nichinyama. If Koche had been a real sister to Nichinyama, then Saidi, at about 30 years old, would have been a sister's son to Nguro and Budzo, who were in their late 50's. But since Koche had been a slave and Saidi was master, the only way of acknowledging his special status while showing their own seniority in age was to refer to him, with honor, as grandchild of the matrilineage. Because alternating generations were equated, making Saidi a child in age and a parent in status, Nguro and Budzo also called him mother's brother, or sometimes, father. The Digo helped to manage their relationships of inequality with complexities in terminology.

We learned about this situation with difficulty, because the Digo did not wish to discuss their inequalities. One day we were invited to be present while Nguro negotiated the final installment of bridewealth payments given for his eldest daughter. Nguro was assisted in this by Budzo Safari who was his matrilateral parallel cousin, hence, 'brother.' A few others were there - including his son Kasim who was the brother of the bride; Selemani Chuo, a friend acting as go-between; and Saidi Bamvua - however, Nguro deferred to Saidi and seemed to hang on his every word. Saidi said that the payments offered by the groom's kin were too small, that it was an insult to the honor of the house. Nguro had been ready to accept them until Saidi showed his displeasure. Selemani Chuo eventually prevailed upon Saidi to agree, but as negotiations were concluded Saidi continued to show that he was influential beyond his years. When we asked the reason for his influence we were only told that he was the grandchild of the matrilineage.

Months later, Nguro was taken ill. Divination revealed that he was being attacked by black magic, hidden somewhere in his homestead or coconut orchard by an ancient enemy. Kin gathered to join the traditional searching out and cleansing of this evil by a noted ritual specialist, then all contributed to pay for the ritual, which was very expensive. Throughout this process, Saidi Bamvua again played a major role, usually sitting back, listening to and watching others; then at a crucial moment, entering and taking charge. He contributed more than any one else. Again we asked for reasons, and again we were told that he was a grandchild of the lineage; a well-intentioned one at that, who displayed proper manners.

In spite of this cleansing, Nguro died. Following tradition, he was to be buried within a day of his death in an elaborate funeral ritual. Normally a senior kinsman was appointed to direct the funeral and the subsequent deliberations about inheritance and succession. Almost everyone agreed that Budzo Safari, Nguro's close parallel cousin, was the logical choice, but Saidi Bamvua claimed the right. Saidi also said that the body should be buried in a graveyard belonging to Chinaniterema, where others of his line were buried, as were those who were slaves and satellites to it. The position of the graves showed the relative rank of the occupants, and buried ancestors and their ghosts validated claims to land and palm orchards.

Some Chinarama of both the line of Niterema and of its sister line agreed with Saidi, but others did not. Omari Malau, a descendent of Nigao senior and a sister's son of Nguro, did a very un-Digo thing by exploding in anger at Saidi's claim. He said that the Chinagao and Chinakoche were no longer to be treated as slaves, and he demanded that the body of Nguro be buried in land long farmed and planted in palms by the Chinagao. It looked as if the various factions would come to blows, again something unusual for the Digo. Budzo Safari offered a compromise; bury the body on land that Nguro himself had cleared and planted. The body already had lain unburied for 32 hours, and the smell was obvious. Everyone agreed that it was disgraceful, so the compromise was accepted. But when the presence of thick tree roots made it very difficult to dig the grave, Saidi said that the ghosts of his lineage and that of Koche were displeased and were rejecting the grave; it had to be moved to the Niterema land. Omari Malau hurriedly had reinforcements brought in to hasten the digging, and eventually Nguro was laid to rest in his land.

Subsequently, some Digo observed that this solution was very clever, because it meant that the close kin of Nguro had made firm their control of Nguro's palms. Saidi Bamvua said that from now on the kin of Nguro were on their own, he would not help them; but other Chinarama sought to keep them in the fold. By establishing control over the burial of their kin as well as the ownership of palms and land of their own, the relatives of Nguro changed their status and seriously challenged the stigma of their slave heritage.

Chifudu and kombolela

Other Digo also were making claims for independence from their master lineage by establishing family curing shrines or redeeming rights in pre-slave lineages. Traditionally the Digo, like many of the peoples from whom they took slaves (Champion 1967, Brantley 1981), sought healing, in part through worship at ancestral shrines that were built like miniature Digo houses. The chifudu is the ritual and medicine used to protect and restore family health and fertility. Traditionally, the women of a senior lineage were organized in a *chifudu* cult under a senior woman, and they participated in regular ritual. Slaves and their descendents could not establish their own shrines, but they were protected by the *chifudu* of their masters. Like burial in lineage land, the organization of these cults showed who was master and who was slave.

By the 1950's, this *chifudu* system had practically vanished. The Digo said that this was because the ritual itself, particularly its songs and dancing, were contrary to Islam; pagan and dirty, it was not something even to discuss. But we saw a shrine being built and its medicines installed for a woman who was descended from slaves. We eventually were told that it was constructed by her husband, his brothers, and her brothers, and that the medicines were installed by a practitioner who knew what was appropriate to her ancestry. The shrine was necessary because divination showed that the woman and her daughters required treatment from it to become well, but clearly, in negotiating the right to build the shrine, the woman and her family also negotiated and symbolized status change. The Digo admitted that a few other women of slave descent achieved much the same compromise in the Lungalunga area in the 1950's. They were allowed to build a shrine, but had to restrict their curing to their collaterals and descendents.

A few Digo who were descended from slaves wanted to go beyond this compromise by redeeming membership in their lost clan. Reincorporation, or *kombolela*, was ritualized in a ceremony of rocking, as a baby is rocked in the arms of its mother. The Digo expected the group that reclaimed them to give them land, coconut palms, and other help in exchange for the strength that they added to it. They also expected those they threatened to leave to give them concessions to remain. For all concerned, honor was at stake as well as people and property. Because some people tried to win on all counts, property transfers occasioned by *kombolela* were sometimes disputed. In one case, a Lungalunga man, Halifani, harvested coconuts from palms planted both by the lineage that had reclaimed him and the lineage he deserted. In time, the deserted lineage took Halifani to District Court to have him vacate his rights in their groves, but they could not effectively argue their case because they did not want to admit to the

British officer that slave descent was at issue. Halifani won by claiming inheritance through the Islamic patrilineal law.

Redemption was unlikely for many of the Digo slaves who had been taken from other, sometimes distant, tribes. When Omari Malau threatened to secede to join his ancestral Doe people and to take his Chinagao with him, the Digo regarded it as an empty threat. The Doe, a small tribe in Tanganyika, had little to offer.

Song contest

Knowing genealogy helped the Digo build and hold networks of supporters, negotiate statuses, and claim rights to coconut palms. Elders regarded knowledge about ancestry to be a valued possession that could be passed on to younger Digo in exchange for aid. One of the ways the Digo remembered their history and ancestry was by couching the information in the form of song and verse.

In the 1950's, there were a few Digo known for their ability to sing parts of these songs as art and entertainment rather than as a recitation of history, but the Digo said that in the 1940's, Digo men representing their lineages fought each other using complete songs about ancestry. The victor was the one who could most clearly show that his ancestry was the purest, and especially that it was master of his rival's lineage. These song contests were potentially disruptive affairs involving much of the population of the Digo district, directly or indirectly. They tore, or threatened to tear, communities and clans apart, in spite of the fact that many Digo recognized everyone's slave or master heritage if their ancestries were traced far enough through both father and mother. Also, the contests were very expensive. Food and drink, including palm wine, were served; elders from other parts of the district came in to judge the singing, and had to be paid; elders who knew ancestral secrets sold these to the highest bidder, perhaps as a way to retain influence in spite of their advancing age and social change.

By the 1950's, the Digo seemed pleased that the contests had ended. The songs and the related drinking were called pagan and dirty, much the same rhetoric that was used to criticize rituals of curing and redemption. Apparently, the Digo once more used Islamic ideology to justify changing some aspect of their past, and applied Islam in various ways to help them manage their social relationships. They used it to suppress recounting of master-slave ancestry in the song contests, but also to suppress rituals of escape from slave heritage that were embodied in the curing and redemption ceremonies. Men, in particular, used it to legitimate patrilineal inheritance while camouflaging slave heritage; women used it to claim shares of bridewealth in order to dramatize their rejection of slave-like treatment; and the Digo as a whole used Islam to help end the rituals that supported age grading and associated hierarchies in the *ngambi*. Through these applications of Islam, the Digo lived more equally, but also more complexly.

Entrepreneurial Digo

Even as the Digo were trying to overcome their history of hierarchy and stratification, they were faced with a new force for inequality. This force was that of their fellow Digo who were becoming entrepreneurs in the production and sale of cash crops, and especially in the growing bicycle-transported trade in fresh fish, vegetables, and milk (Gerlach 1963). The entrepreneurs, chiefly young men, were earning cash through this business that enabled them to gain power over others by investing it in new as well as traditional ways. The Digo had been involved in coastal trading over their history, but in the 1950's this enterprise was greatly magnified by innovations in marketing. Because fish and milk spoiled if carried by foot from coastal ports or cattle country to Digo farming villages, traditionally most Digo settled for wild greens or dried fish to prepare the sauce for customary meals of maize or cassava porridge and prepared tea with tinned milk, if they used milk at all. A few entrepreneurs found that if they carried these wares by bicycle, with the fish wrapped in wet burlap, the produce could be sold fresh. Soon others followed, and many prospered as they traversed different ecological zones buying and selling vegetables, fish, and milk according to opportunity and demand (Gerlach 1963, 1965).

Entrepreneurs found that Digo pride, ideas of equality, and social-support networks could be applied to help their enterprise. As some women obtained fish and milk from their husbands and brothers, other women were provoked by envy to demand the same from their menfolk. Word spread among the Digo women that it was animal-like, slave-like, to use wild greens to make sauces for maize porridge; they were demeaned if their men did not provide them with fresh fish.

Entrepreneurs obtained their starting capital by growing and selling cash crops and by working in cities for wages. They secured their operating and maintenance capital by reinvesting the profits from sales. This capital was their most vital asset, and their main problem was to protect it from the customary pressures to share while maintaining the good will of other Digo. Egalitarian values were a help to entrepreneurs, who used them to secure more personal freedom to pursue business and to motivate other Digo to buy their products in order to keep up with the neighbors. But these values also were a hindrance to businessmen when the Digo, who envied the entrepreneurs their success and feared their rise to wealth and potential dominance, used ideas of equality and collectivism to block them.

The entrepreneurs' problem was illustrated as we watched Hassani Fumbwe, one of the most successful traders, prepare and sell his fish in the Lungalunga village square. Juma, his *awu* or mother's brother, joined the crowd of customers, all of whom were men. Juma, who spoke Digo throughout the exchange, instead of buying, coaxed Hassani to give him some free fish as befitted a *muwa*, or sister's son. For many minutes, Hassani ignored Juma but continued his sales using the Swahili language. Finally he said, still in Swahili: 'uncle (*mjomba*), in business there is no mother's brother (*awu*).' He called Juma by the Swahili term *mjomba* because it meant either father's or mother's brother, and thereby ignored the special mother's brother/sister's son relationship that united them under other circumstances. While Juma accepted this statement, he expected that in other contexts Hassani would help him. For example, Hassani had sought not to contribute to a traditional curing ritual that he called pagan and backward. Instead, Juma and other kin asked him to meet a modern need by paying school fees for their children. Hassani agreed, but asked that some of these young kin live with him to help him and his wife farm their land, and with this assistance he was able to grow cash crops.

The pressure to share put the Digo businessman in a double bind. If he did not help, he was considered to be selfish and to be evading his duties. However, if he became a consistent source of aid to people, they would become obligated to him and eventually resent his power. In either case, he became a target of trouble-making gossip. Finding an appropriate balance was as much a test of entrepreneurship as buying cheap and selling dear or convincing the Digo to use fresh fish and milk.

The main way Digo businessmen responded to pressures to share was to tie up their fluid cash in granting *rahani* loans to senior Digo who managed coconut groves. Then, when asked for contributions, entrepreneurs said they could not offer anything unless the *rahani* loan was repaid them; they had no cash. Typically the loan could not be repaid on demand because the borrower had not reinvested it in a money-making business, but usually had used it in more traditional pursuits; to pay for ritual curing, for bridewealth, or to settle a divorce. As Muslims, they could not take direct interest on the loan, but Digo creditors profited by producing and selling copra from the groves until the debt was repaid.

Acting as good neighbors or kin, entrepreneurs continued giving loans and using the mortgaged palms. On one hand, based on their control of this major Digo resource, entrepreneurs potentially could threaten their fellows with a new structure of stratification. On the other hand, entrepreneurs were a source of Digo pride as they demonstrated that the Digo could prosper in business and compete against Arab and Indian merchants. Consequently, to preserve equality, the Digo were challenged to manage the businessman as both asset and threat.

Just as the original traders on bicycles improved their own financial position while enabling their fellows to diversify their diets, a combination of individual interest with Digo practices of equality and group ownership sometimes benefited everyone. Some of the Digo businessmen teamed up with young Digo political activists to develop people's cooperatives for marketing copra and other cash crops independently of the Asians. The cooperative promoters promised their members higher financial returns as well as pride of ownership, and successfully maintained a balance between individual pride and group responsibility.

Rituals of reciprocity

In the 1950's, the Digo were making considerable use of ritual to manage possessing spirits, and this ritual subsequently helped them to control both the new and the enduring threats to their social system. They were able to distribute power

134

and wealth more evenly, essentially by enabling relatively deprived or threatened women and men to express their problems and objectives through the voice of spirits. The system also enabled the Digo to validate their membership in property-sharing and other groups through personal contributions to members of these groups who required ritual assistance. Validating his membership in a group in this way also ensured that an individual would be helped by the other members in his own time of need. The Digo used the ritual to make change, and to control and adapt to change.

To their own pantheon of supernatural beings, the Digo added several acquired through Arabic-Islamic influence. By recognizing so many types of spirits, each with different origins, roles, demands, and treatments, the Digo followed their usual way of incorporating cultural alternatives. Women were the main hosts of the spirits, who were attracted by 'sweet blood,' but men, usually those beset by other troubles, also could be hosts.

Patterns like these are reported for other peoples in Africa, and spirit possession is usually explained as a response to psychological or social stress (Harris 1978) or deprivation (Lewis 1966, 1967); but the management of possessing spirits was much more than a religion of the deprived. As Giles (1987) theorizes, for people sharing Swahili culture generally, including the Digo, spirit possession can fulfill many different functions depending on the circumstances. One major function is that of symbolic expression. Possession helps reveal the many conceptual oppositions in complex Swahili society, reflecting its history of culture contact and change. For the Digo, the oppositions were between Islamic and non-Islamic or pagan culture, between matrilineal and patrilineal organization, and between hierarchy and egalitarianism or mastery and slavery. Possession not only symbolically revealed these oppositions, it helped the Digo manage them.

Possession by spirits could make the hosts mentally or physically ill, unable to have children, or hostile to a husband's sexual advances. Spirits took revenge if they had been angered, perhaps when their host had been mistreated by kin or affines. Spirits' anger also could easily spill over to hurt others, particularly the children of the host.

Troubled by this potential danger, men close to the sick woman took her case to a diviner who would identify the spirit or spirits involved and recommend a curer who could call up and deal with these particular spirits in a ceremony.

It was up to the male kin and affines of the sick woman to arrange this ritual, to attend it, and to pay for it. During the curing ceremony both the curer and the host went into trance. The spirits of the curer engaged in long discourse with the spirits of the woman who spoke through the mouth of their host, and who were able say things with a frankness the Digo could not otherwise employ. Usually spirits blamed close kin or her husband for mistreating a woman, chiefly by not supporting her in material, social, and emotional ways. In time the curer, either as a person or as a medium, negotiated settlements with the spirits of the woman and her relatives, both those spirits who had troubled her and those who should have protected her.

Settlements usually included granting the woman material items - chiefly clothing, utensils, a goat to herd - as well as the promise of a major ritual of drumming and dancing to please the spirits. Through such a ritual, the woman was helped to gain control over her spirits so that they would assist instead of harm her. She was joined in both curing ceremony and restorative ritual by other women who had been involved with similar spirits and handled by the same curer. And she then was able to join these women in an association devoted to managing their spirits.

All of this was very expensive and time consuming for those who supported the woman. If men did not give such support to their wives or kinswomen, they would certainly lose prestige. They also would be accused of not fulfilling their obligations as managers of group property, or worse, of trying to kill the woman. So people contributed, often both with respect to the closeness of their relationship with the possessed woman and with their ability to pay. Managers of group coconut groves were expected to use the copra or the *rahani* from the groves to raise curing funds, either to contribute themselves or to give to group members to contribute. Thus, curing rituals promoted a broader circulation of wealth from group property, just as it enabled sharers to validate their various rights to the property. Yet, even as it was used to encourage participation in collectivities, curing ritual also helped individuals, male and female, to gain some independence of action. It helped a woman to counter both the new Islamic power of men and their traditional power, not only collectively as a member of spirit associations, but personally, by negotiating a more satisfactory relationship with the men and women in her life. Digo men and women also legitimated their individualism as a response to the demands of new spirits. Parkin (1972) reports a somewhat similar pattern among the Giriama where the entrepreneurs converted to Islam to be cured of spirit illnesses, then used their new religion as a reason not to contribute to expensive traditional religious events.

Digo curing ritual was, of course, a source of wealth and power to its ritual specialists who had considerable influence over their patients and the spirit associations. The more Islamic the spirits, the more likely it was that these specialists would be men. One curer near Lungalunga mobilized his spirit association to help his son run for political office in the newly independent Kenya. He and a curer in Lungalunga helped to form the copra and fish marketing cooperative that was mentioned in the last section, and his influence helped one of his male patients become chief of a Digo location in the late 1970's. Of course, ritual specialists themselves were controlled by the criticisms of their fellow Digo. They were particularly subject to the rumor that they not only practiced curing ritual, which was good, but that they also used black magic. The Digo curing ritual, then, was an institution that contributed complexly and variously to Digo efforts to manage the tensions between individualism and collectivism in ways that produced their uneasy egalitarianism.

Conclusion

The management of possessing spirits was one of the Digo institutions that the colonial officials most denigrated, because they felt that it was backward and wasted wealth. They wanted to eliminate it, just as they wanted the Digo to simplify their system of inheritance and to use their land more productively. Some felt that the Digo would be more productive if they cooperated more effectively under strong leadership, such as they were reported to have done in their past when the *ngambi* was hierarchical. Other officials felt that the Digo would be more productive if they privatized their tenure of land and coconut palms, and farmed their land as small holders.

The colonial administration was promoting both privatization and hierarchically organized cooperation among the Nandi, Kamba, and other landless peoples from up-country Kenya whom the administration had resettled in a large block of government land in the Shimba Hills near Kwale (Palmer 1971). Administrators urged the Digo to enter the project. They declined, politely but persistently, (even as they complained that it was wrong for the government to give others land that once had belonged to the Digo). The Digo said that they did not enter the project because the land was beset with evil spirits; but as much as anything else, they did not want to be subject to project rules and officials. They felt that the settlers sacrificed their pride to obtain land, and some also worried that much of the land was too dry to establish coconut orchards.

In Lungalunga, the Digo also declined to take up government offers to plant new strains of coconut palms that were more productive, shorter, easier to climb and harvest, and disease resistant. In order to qualify for government help in planting these new trees, the Digo would have had to have their land surveyed and to use it as security for no-interest government loans. These two conditions, along with the slow replacement of their old, sometimes dying, palms with the new seedlings, threatened to bring into conflict the various contesting heirs to coconut groves and to demolish the compromise groups. In one instance, the heirs on the male side did seek to accept the government offer; they were persuaded by the community to reestablish compromise with the female side and to ritualize this agreement by placating the spirit of their common ancestors.

Time and again, the Digo rather politely listened to colonial administrators harangue them in public meetings for not participating in these modernization and development projects, for not clarifying their rules of inheritance and succession, for not cooperating under a stronger leader, for not preparing themselves for eventual self government. The Digo agreed they were a problem. They explained their inability to cooperate with the government with an old Swahili saying, attributed to the Arabs who once ruled the coast:

Digo Mzigo
Hachakuliki

The Digo is a burden
He cannot be carried.

It seems to us that by using this saying, the Digo appeared simplistic, when, in fact, they had a very complex system.

The Digo were complex because of the ways in which they were changing and adapting to change. Their system was baffling and troubling to outsiders, but though it was complex, it was not confusing to the Digo. They incorporated various contradictory rules derived from different cultural sources, not because they were unable to control change, but because these diverse rules provided them with the use of a range of cultural alternatives to accomplish their objectives in the face of colonial domination.

The Digo applied these rules and processes in ways that consistently resulted in a condition we can term egalitarianism; social, economic and political. This egalitarianism, we argue, was less the Digo purpose than the result of the way the Digo used and sought to promote sharing while preventing donors from making recipients into subordinates. Egalitarianism was a product of the tension between collectivism and individualism in Digo culture that, in turn, was shaped by their earlier history of slave holding, stratification, and hierarchy.

Notes

[1] The authors conducted the initial research for this study
     from 1958-1960 under the Fulbright Fellowship Program.
     They obtained additional data in 1983/1984 under a Bush
     Sabbatical Fellowship, and were afforded the opportunity
     to write this essay in the summer of 1986 under a visiting
     fellowship at the International Institute for Environment
     and Society, The Science Center, West Berlin.

     The authors wish to thank these fellowship programs for
     their assistance, and Patricia Lund for her help in editing
     this final draft.

Bibliography

Anderson, J.N.D. 1954. *Islamic Law in Africa.* Colonial Research Publications #16. London: Her Majesty's Stationery Office.

Bohannan, Paul 1963. *Social Anthropology.* New York: Holt, Rinehart and Winston, Inc.

Brantley, Cynthia 1981. *The Giriama and Colonial Resistance in Kenya, 1800-1920.* Berkeley: University of California Press.

Champion, A.M. 1967. *The Agiriama of Kenya* (ed) John Middleton. London: Occasional Paper 25, Royal Anthropological Institute.

Comaroff, John 1980. 'Introduction.' In *The Meaning of Marriage Payments, Studies in Anthropology* (ed) John Comaroff. New York: Academic Press.

Cotran, Eugene 1969. 'The Digo.' Chapter 9 in *The Law of Succession, Kenya II, Restatement of African Law: 2.* London: Sweet and Maxwell.

Coupland, Reginald 1965. *East Africa and Its Invaders.* New York: Russell & Russell, Inc.

Evans-Pritchard, E.E. 1940. *The Nuer.* Oxford, London: Oxford University Press.

Evans-Pritchard, E.E. 1940a. 'The Nuer of the Southern Sudan.' In *African Political Systems* (eds) M. Fortes and E.E. Evans-Pritchard. London, New York: International African Institute, Oxford University Press.

Forde, C.D. 1950. 'Double Descent Among the Yako.' In *African Systems of Kinship and Marriage* (eds) A.R. Radcliffe-Brown and D. Forde. London: International African Institute, Oxford University Press.

Forde, C.D. 1964. *Yako Studies.* Oxford: Oxford University Press.

Fortes, M. and E.E. Evans-Pritchard 1940. *African Political Systems*. London, New York: International African Institute, Oxford University Press.

Gerlach, Luther P. 1963. 'Traders on Bicycles: A Study of Entrepreneurship and Culture Change Among the Digo and Duruma of Kenya.' In *Sociologus YIII, I*, 32-49.

Gerlach, Luther P. 1965. 'Nutrition in its Sociocultural Matrix: Food Getting and Using Along the East African Coast.' In *Ecology and Economic Development in Tropical Africa* (ed) David Brokensha. Berkeley: Research Series No. 9, Institute of International Studies, University of California.

Giles, Linda L. 1987. 'Possession Cults on the Swahili Coast: A Re-examination of Theories of Marginality.' In *Africa, Journal of the International African Institute*.

Gomm, R. 1972. 'Harlots and Bachelors; Marital Instability Among the Coastal Digo of Kenya.' In *MAN*, (ns) 7, 4, 95-113.

Harris, Grace Gredys 1978. *Casting Out Anger: Religion Among the Taita of Kenya*. Cambridge: Cambridge University Press.

Lewis, I.M. 1966. 'Spirit Possession and Deprivation Cults.' In *Man*, 1(3), 307-29.

Lewis, I.M. 1967. 'Spirits and the Sex War.' In *Man*, 2(4), 626-28.

Mair, Lucy 1962, revised 1977. *Primitive Government*. Bloomington: Indiana University Press.

Middleton, John and David Tait (eds) 1958. *Tribes Without Rulers*. London: Routledge & Kegan Paul.

Murdock, George Peter 1959. *Africa: Its Peoples and Their Culture History*. Toronto & London: McGraw-Hill Book Co.

New, Charles 1971. *Life, Wanderings, and Labours in Eastern Africa*. London: Frank Cass & Co. Ltd.

Palmer, Gary 1971. 'The Shimba Hills Settlement Scheme: The Administration of Large Scale Innovation in Kenya.' Unpublished PhD dissertation, University of Minnesota.

Parkin, David J. 1972. *Palms, Wine and Witness: Public Spirit and Private Gain in an African Community.* San Francisco: Chandler Publishing Co.

Parkin, David J. 1980. 'Kind Bridewealth and Hard Cash: Eventing a Structure.' In *The Meaning of Marriage Payments* (ed) John Comaroff. New York: Academic Press.

Prins, A.H.H. 1952. 'The Coastal Tribes of the North-Eastern Bantu.' In *Ethnographic Survey of Africa* (ed) Daryll Forde. London: International African Institute.

Salim, Ahmed Idha 1976. 'Native or Non-native? The Problem of Identity and the Social Stratification of the Arab Swahili of Kenya.' In *History and Social Change in East Africa* (ed) Bethwell A. Ogot. Nairobi: East African Publishing House.

Schneider, Harold K. 1981. *The Africans: An Ethnological Account.* New Jersey: Prentice-Hall, Inc.

Service, Elman 1975. *Origins of the State and Civilization.* New York: Random House.

Spear, Thomas J. 1976. 'The Mijikenda, 1550-1900.' In *Kenya Before 1900* (ed) Bethwell A. Ogot. Nairobi: East African Publishing House.

Spear, Thomas J. 1981. *Kenya's Past: An Introduction to Historical Method in Africa.* London: Longman Group Ltd.

Spiro, Melford 1975. 'Marriage Payments: A Paradigm from the Burmese Perspective.' In *Journal of Anthropological Research* 31, 89-115.

Trigger, Bruce 1985. 'Generalized Coercion and Inequality: The Basis of State Power in the Early Civilizations.' In *Development and Decline: The Evolution of Sociopolitical Organization* (eds) Henri J.M. Claessen, Pieter van de Velde and M. Estellie Smith. Massachussetts: Bergin and Garvey Publishers, Inc.

143

Trimmingham, J. Spencer 1962. *Islam in East Africa.* London: Research Pamphlet No. 9, Edinburgh House Press.

Turner, Victor W. 1957. *Schism and Continuity in an African Society: A Study of Ndembu Village Life.* Manchester: Manchester University Press, Institute for African Studies, University of Zambia.

Warren, D.E. 1962. *Atlas of Kenya.* Nairobi, Kenya: The Survey of Kenya 1962.

7 Context and community: equality and social change on a Polynesian outlier

WILLIAM DONNER

ABSTRACT

The character of social relationships on a Polynesian outlier is examined, and the dynamics of such relationships in undifferentiated social organizations are compared with those of complex differentiated societies. Based on extensive fieldwork on Sikaiana, the paper explores the social contexts that express and reinforce egalitarian values including: (1) the indigenous institutions of kinship, descent, fosterage, and ritual; (2) interaction routines such as ridicule and gossip; and (3) the recently introduced western institutions of church, school, and court.

Introduction

My perspective on equality is shaped by interactional approaches to social relationships that examine individuals in their roles and encounters.[1] A person is a member of many different social categories (or roles), each with its distinct entitlements, obligations, rights, duties, and expectations about appropriate behavior change, depending upon the social setting, institutional context, and role. Only some social categories are relevant in any particular social relationship or setting, although, as Goffman (1961) argued in his discussion of role distance, behavior is sometimes manipulated to express obligations to a variety of settings and roles. This paper describes the contexts for egalitarian relationships on Sikaiana, a Polynesian outlier located in the Solomon Islands.[2]

In some complex societies, universal and impersonal social categories define people as equals in certain matters. For example, both in the Solomon Islands and the United States, a large number of people consider themselves to have the same entitlements as members of universalistic religious organizations, that is, they are equal before God. They also share equal entitlements as citizens of the national polity, possessing some basic rights in the courts and at the polls. Industrial societies are often depicted as being stratified according to distinctions determined by wealth, power and prestige. To be sure, there are differences between people (and, perhaps, classes of people) in terms of their economic and political control over others; but there is a certain equality in terms of the abstract universalistic categories discussed above, although people disagree about the relevance of the categories for a person's life chances.

Moreover, power, authority, and influence change depending upon context. In their places of employment, the boss and employee, who are equals in terms of the highly abstract categories mentioned above, are not equal. Nevertheless, in our society, subordinates and superordinates may find their relationships reversed depending upon the social setting (see Simmel 1950:285). In time of war, for example, the wealthy may find themselves taking orders from men who in peacetime are their servants. Equality must be examined in its various social contexts, and labeling a society as egalitarian or not often depends upon the contexts that are selected for study. This perspective on social relationships, interactions, and contexts is the basis for my discussion of egalitarian social relationships on Sikaiana.

There are important respects in which Sikaiana social relationships are unequal. Generally, older people have entitlements that give them prerogatives over younger people. In public affairs and the control of resources, males usually have entitlements that make them dominant over females. Although small in population and comparatively undifferentiated in role specialization, Sikaiana has many different

146

settings in which people possess, at least temporarily, unequal power, authority, and influence.

Nevertheless, I consider Sikaiana to be an egalitarian society in many respects,[3] since there is an ideology about social relationships that is egalitarian. This ideology is grounded in a decentralized system of land tenure, and because Sikaiana is a kinship-based society, many of its egalitarian features are kinship based. For instance, there are high rates of fosterage among kin that create emotional ties and mitigate any incipient social stratification. Another social context for equality and conviviality is drinking fermented toddy, the major festive activity on Sikaiana. Finally, on the atoll, many different individuals participate in the institutions that manage its affairs, and there is comparatively little differentiation and specialization in roles.

Background

Sikaiana is an atoll located about 100 miles east of Malaita Island in the Solomon Islands. The Solomon Islands, formerly a British Protectorate, is a nation including many different cultural and social groups, most of which are Melanesian and Polynesian. In their traditions, language, and culture, the Sikaiana are Polynesian and have many similarities with other peoples in West Polynesia, including those of Samoa, Tuvalu (Ellice Islands), Ontong Java and Tikopia. Like its neighbors in Polynesia and Melanesia, Sikaiana has experienced dramatic culture change in the 20th century as a result of contact with European traders, missionaries, and Protectorate officials. Much of the traditional technology has been replaced by western trade goods including axes, kerosene lanterns, clothing, cookware, imported fishing equipment, and manufactured housing materials. The Christian church, a local court, schools, and a locally elected government are important institutions on present-day Sikaiana. Many Sikaiana adults are employed for wages in western occupations such as clerks, laborers, administrators, and other specialities. Almost every Sikaiana person is fluent in Pidgin English, the lingua franca of the Solomon Islands, and some are fluent in English. Although these are dramatic changes in Sikaiana society, the Sikaiana people have retained many traditional values and preserved themselves as a distinct ethnic group and community in the Solomon Islands (Donner 1985).

In the early 20th century, Sikaiana had a resident population of about 200-250 people. Following the arrival of Anglican missionaries in 1929, the population increased rapidly (probably as a result of improved health conditions and the missionaries' prohibition of abortion.) At the same time, the missionaries and the Protectorate government offered opportunities for emigration from the atoll to other areas of the Solomon Islands. People began leaving to work for wages, and children left to attend mission schools. After the Second World War, emigration increased. At present, the number of residents on the atoll fluctuates at about 200-250 residents, with about 400-450 other Sikaiana people living in other parts of the Solomon Islands. Most of the emigrants maintain important ties with other Sikaiana people, and they still think of the atoll as their home. Residents living in and around Honiara often participate together in festive events and weddings. There is a strong preference for marriage with other Sikaiana people, although there are increasing numbers of marriages with other ethnic groups in the Solomon Islands.

In the following discussion, egalitarian relationships in present-day Sikaiana society will be discussed. I will begin with an examination of cultural expectations about individual behavior and proper etiquette in social interaction, and then describe various contexts and mechanisms for egalitarian relationships including rights to use land, fosterage, toddy drinking, and widespread participation in the atoll's offices, committees, and decision making. The conclusion will examine these egalitarian relationships in terms of the small size of the Sikaiana community and its integration into a more complex, multi-ethnic, regional social system. To repeat a point made earlier, though there are many ways in which the Sikaiana are unequal, the following discussion focuses on the relationships, settings, and contexts that are equal, and the senses in which I consider their community to be egalitarian.

Equality in persons and interpersonal etiquette

Sikaiana concepts about individual character and proper etiquette for social interaction support egalitarianism in social relationships (see Beteille 1986). In speaking abstractly, a Sikaiana person will emphasize that people should be treated as 'equal' or 'the same' (*naatahi*). Ideally, Sikaiana social interaction is based upon harmony, agreement, and humility.

The compound term *hakapaapaalalo* is sometimes used to describe proper humility in social behavior. *Paapaa* is the word 'to be flat'; *lalo* means 'below'. *Hakapaapaalalo* literally means 'to make flat to below'. Although a Sikaiana person does not bow, crawl, or lie flat in normal social interaction, this word reflects concern with humility and restraint. *Kkolu* is a verb that is frequently used in criticism to describe a person who is trying to force his/her way or prevail over others in social relationships. *Kkolu* also describes the behavior of young children who insist upon having their way, especially when they go into a tantrum. When used with inanimate nouns, such as metal objects, *kkolu* means 'to bend,' especially as in bending a hard substance like steel. In proper social interaction, a person should not try to force or bend the behavior or opinions of others.

The Sikaiana people know one another as individuals with unique personalities and life histories. This individuality is an important source for gossip, conversation, and joking. Unusual, excessive, or idiosyncratic behavior is ridiculed and discouraged. Distinctive physical characteristics, such as blinking, jerking the neck, or twitching are described as a *maapu*, and there is joking and teasing about these traits. The meaning of *maapu* is extended to include unusual habits or characteristics. Special terms are used to ridicule over-indulgence: a person who eats too much, *haakai*; a person who smokes too much, *saa mmiti*; a person who drinks too much fermented toddy, *saa kaleve*; a baby who nurses too much, *saa uu* or *sina uu*. Other kinds of idiosyncracies are ridiculed, such as unusual styles of dancing and dressing, or affecting a European life style.

Individuals should not show off or behave in ways that draw attention to themselves. Modesty is especially important for young women who are discouraged from loud behavior or being overly coquettish. The causative prefix, *haka-* is affixed to the words for 'woman' *hahine*, and 'man' *tanata*, to describe the action of 'showing off in a feminine manner' *hakahahine*, and 'showing off in a masculine manner' *hakatanata*. These terms are frequently used to ridicule young people who try to attract attention to themselves. Indeed, humility is implicit in the etymology of a common term for 'praise,' *hakanapa*. *Napa* is the word for 'shame' and *haka-* is the causative prefix. *Hakanapa* could be literally translated as 'to cause to be ashamed', but usually has the meaning of 'to praise'. Praise, by calling attention to the individual, causes embarrassment for the Sikaiana person.

These expectations about restraint and humility in social relationships affect leadership. There are several Sikaiana men who, through their achievements and personality, are highly respected and influential within the community. During my stay, they included the atoll's priest, a doctor, and a government official. Each of these men had been successful in schools, received advanced training in some speciality, and helped the Sikaiana people in his respective institution: religion, medicine, or the government. Although these men are influential, they are reluctant to force their will on others, and they are restrained in asserting their influence. One of these men was elected to the local government council, but he did not stand for president of that council, although I am almost certain he would have been elected had he chosen to do so. During my stay, the priest did not participate in any of the atoll's committees or offices, other than those associated with the church.

Periodically, there are meetings of Sikaiana's residents to discuss various projects or matters of concern. At these meetings, there are efforts to reach a public consensus before proceeding on any project. A project is likely to find indifference and opposition if it is introduced without the prior participation and consent of the atoll's residents. Important issues affecting the entire population are discussed in separate meetings by residents of Sikaiana, and again by the Sikaiana residents of Honiara. The members of the local government council try to base their decisions upon consensus, although there is an undercurrent of friction between various factions within the community. In most cases, the justices of the local court discuss an issue until a consensus is reached before giving their verdict.

Land rights

Sikaiana equality is also reflected in rights to a major resource, land. In many cases, rights to land are possessed by the patrilineal descendants of the person who originally acquired rights to the land.[4] Non-agnatic offspring have rights to use the lineage's land, but they may be expelled if they offend the agnatic male members of the lineage. After several generations, the descendants of a female link tend to use the lineage's land less frequently (unless rights to use this land have been formally transferred to these descendants). Most Sikaiana males have inalienable rights to some tracts of land through agnatic links. At present, it is virtually impossible to expel a male patrilineal descendant of the lineage's founder. As a result of the population rise of the last 50 years, there are many more members within each lineage than in previous times. Nevertheless, lineages have not segmented, and descendants retain rights to their lineage's land.

There are no formal meetings of lineages to discuss their affairs; decisions are based upon the mutual consent of older members. Normally, younger people should defer to older people, and females should defer to males; but other factors, such as knowledge of lineage affairs, affect a person's influence, so, in some cases, younger males and females are very influential in a lineage's decisions.

In most lineages, there is one person, always male, who is identifiable as a spokesman, and who represents his lineage in land disputes and court cases. These men should be familiar with genealogies, lineage history, and the court system. Often, they are not the oldest in their lineages, rather, they are middle-aged men who are familiar with the government's court system. They also should be forceful men who are not afraid to face the hostilities caused by court disputes.

This system of land tenure is quite distinctive from other hierarchically organized Polynesian societies where a chiefly line has rights of eminent domain over land used by other people.[5] It is also quite distinctive from other non-unilineal systems of tenure where land rights are redistributed every few generations.[6]

Fosterage

Fosterage, the transfer of children between different households and establishment of emotional ties across a broad range of kin, is an important mechanism for maintaining egalitarian relationships. Fostering non-natal children is normative, both as a statistical frequency and as an ideal value. In my household census for 1981, 48% of the children on Sikaiana were residing with their foster parents. This figure does not reflect the full extent of fosterage, because many children move between several households, including those of their natal parents. Normally, fosterage occurs between extended kin. Often, people claim that it is preferable if the child is a little distant in genealogy and non-agnatically related, since fosterage serves to reinforce kinship ties that are becoming distant. A parent should not refuse a request to take his/her child for fosterage, and it is embarrassing or shameful to demand the return of a child. Many children spend time with both their natal and their foster parents; moreover, they may have several different foster parents with differing levels of involvement.

The child is expected to feel a life-long obligation and commitment to his/her foster parents based upon their support and feeding (*haanai*). The foster child, however, also has obligations to his/her natal parents, and derives his/her land rights and kinship status from them.

In raising children, people claim that all of them, both natal and fostered, should be treated equally. Some people claim that foster parents are more indulgent with their foster children, in some cases spoiling them. I observed no obvious differences in the treatment of foster and natural children. In every family with which I lived, the focus of attention is the youngest child, whether it is a foster child or a natal child.

Fosterage reinforces extended kinship ties, and is a mechanism for mitigating economic differentiation between families.

Toddy drinking

Drinking fermented coconut toddy is an event that is frequent, associated with ceremonial occasions, and standardized in its formalities for participation and distribution.[7] The etiquette and ritual of toddy distribution has similarities with traditional conventions for distributing kava that are recorded in other Polynesian societies. However, kava distribution reflects prestige and rank differences between the participants in many societies; on Sikaiana, toddy distribution reflects egalitarian values. Often, drinking is done in areas that are visible from the main path, and anyone can join a toddy drinking group. People sit in a circle around the container of fermented toddy and the distributor (*taki*), usually the man who fermented the toddy. He pours the toddy into a cup, passes the cup to someone in the group who drinks it, usually in one draught, and returns the cup. Another portion of equal amount is poured and given to the next person in the group. The process is repeated until everyone in the group has a turn. The distributor may vary the size of portions at his discretion, but he should be consistent in distributing the same portion to everyone during each round.

The most enthusiastic drinking occurs during the Sikaiana holidays: Christmas, New Year's, Easter, and on the week devoted to St. Andrew, the patron saint of the Sikaiana church. Most of the adult population, including women, drink in several large groups for several days. In Honiara, on holidays and weddings, Sikaiana emigrants gather together to celebrate and drink, although beer is drunk instead of toddy.

Drinking occasions incorporate most of the community in a secular, festive event. The conventions for participation and distribution involve people as equals with other members of the community. Moreover, by participating in these events, a person takes his equal chances to be subject to insults, quarrels, and fights that are the result of lowered inhibitions. A person who joins in toddy drinking, and almost all residents of Sikaiana participate in holiday drinking, demonstrates commitment to the community.

Social individuation and participation in community affairs

Another important indication that Sikaiana is an egalitarian society is a large degree of participation in the atoll's offices and roles.[8] Before the arrival of the missionaries in 1929, there were many ceremonial offices associated with maintaining the ritual cycle. There are two classes of patrilineal clans: three 'chiefly clans,' (*heto aliki* or *mata aliki*) and four 'commoner clans' (*tanta vale*). The first claim descent from the atoll's founder heroes, Tehui Atahu and Tehui Luaniua, and formerly had the right to succeed to the chieftainship (*aliki*). The latter claimed patrilineal descent from male founders who immigrated to Sikaiana after its original settlement. Members of the chiefly clans proudly claim their descent from the original founders of the atoll; however they do not receive any special interpersonal deference.

These class distinctions seem to have made little difference in the social relationships of pre-Christian Sikaiana society. Elderly people who remember Sikaiana life before the arrival of the missionaries described the chieftaincy as an office that performed the ritual ceremonies necessary to maintain the atoll's welfare. They claim that the chief never had the authority to enter into interpersonal disputes; the parties involved settled the disputes among themselves.[9]

Before the arrival of the missionaries, traditional ritual offices were decentralized, and involved the participation of many different people. The chieftaincy was not consolidated within any single clan, rather the three chiefly clans alternated in succession to the chieftaincy. Moreover, considering the atoll's small population, there were many ritual offices. The chief had several ceremonial assistants (a *taumunimuni, tautuku, tama tootoo hekau,* and two *pule*), and the successor to the chief, *takala,* was a member of a different clan with a different set of men who occupied these ceremonial offices. When the chief died, the *takala* took office as the new chief, and new men succeeded to all of the ritual offices. Although they did not necessarily occupy the offices associated with the atoll's ritual ceremonies, other men also are remembered for being ritually powerful as a result of their contact with the spirits of deceased ancestors.

In the 1930s, the British administration appointed the son of the former *aliki* ('chief') to act as their local representative and the headman. This selection did not follow the traditional line of succession for *aliki*; he should have come from a different clan. Moreover, the British administrators expected him to perform secular political functions that were not part of the traditional role of *aliki*. There were continuing entries in the reports of visiting British administrators describing the tensions between the appointed leaders and the Sikaiana people, resulting in several changes of appointment. During my stay in 1980-83, this position was honorary, and the chief, or headman, had no legitimate political authority, although, depending upon his personality, he might have some degree of influence.

Widespread participation continues in the new offices and specialized roles associated with the western institutions that have been established in the past 50 years. These new offices and roles include catechists, court justices, a court clerk, council members, copra graders, cooperative store clerks, medical dressers or nurses, a radio operator, and a provincial assembly representative. There is also a plethora of committees that support the activities of the atoll's institutions: the Companions (a religious organization for men), the Mother's Union (a religious organization for women), the Club (an organization of the island's women), the Cooperative Store

Committee, the Church Committee, the School Committee, the Kindergarten Committee, among others. Most people participate in one or more of these clubs and committees. Few of the offices require more than minimal, if any, specialized training. The same man may consecutively occupy several different offices, and serve on several different committees; for example, he may be a catechist, a provincial assembly representative, a teacher in the local school, and a justice on the local court. The large number of committees and widespread participation decentralizes the authority system on the atoll, and reinforces the community participation in decision making.

Summary: scale, equality, and changing social relationships

Sikaiana egalitarianism can be understood as an adaptation to the atoll's small population and limited economic resources. In a comparative review of Polynesian social stratification, Sahlins noted that on the stratified Polynesian high islands, 'the essential adaptive problem... was that concerning the economic distribution of large amounts of surplus production (1958:234).' He contrasts this with the situation on low islands, such as Sikaiana, where 'more important was the problem of keeping a dense population alive in an area of sporadic or limited-surplus production (1958:236).' These low islands (including atolls) with limited resources redistribute goods through reciprocal, interlocking, and often egalitarian social relationships (1958:236).

On Sikaiana, these interlocking social relationships must also be understood in terms of the community's small population and lack of role specialization. Most adults have the basic skills necessary to participate in many of the community's roles and institutions: an adult male is house builder, toddy collector, fisherman, canoe builder, council member, copra grader; a female is a cook, gardener, weaver, and shopkeeper. Moreover, the Sikaiana people are part of a dense network of interlocking kinship and personal relationships. Almost the entire adult population is known as distinct individuals, each of whom has accumulated a unique life history, biography, and social ties known to all other members of the community. Everyone is equal before the gossip, ridicule, joking, and personal knowledge that make up much of the social interaction.

155

Sikaiana, however, is becoming integrated into a national, and indeed, a world-wide, economic and political system (see Beteille 1986 for a discussion of similar issues in another social system). In the last 50 years, new social categories such as Christian and citizen have made the Sikaiana people equal with one another in new ways, and established new relationships with members of other ethnic groups in the Solomon Islands where they previously had none. There also are new differences in education, occupation, and wealth that are making Sikaiana unequal in other respects.

The Sikaiana community remains cohesive, and there are still strong norms for interpersonal humility and equality, although there is some indication that the community may differentiate in a manner that will affect its egalitarian relationships. On the atoll, there is still participation in the institutions and roles that administer the community, but the need for specialization and professional certification in some of the atoll's occupational roles such as teacher, priest, and medical practitioner are causing increased differentiation in social relationships. Also, migrants earn different salaries. Eventually, these differences may create new types of inequalities, and undermine the egalitarian features of Sikaiana social organization.

There are further indications of change. According to the Sikaiana people, toddy drinking is heavier now than in previous times. Perhaps this increase in toddy drinking is due in part to a desire to create contexts for egalitarian inter-action in a social system that is incorporating new unequal relationships (see Donner ms).

Fosterage continues to reinforce egalitarianism in a social system that is beginning to develop some distinctions based upon salary differences. The children of both wealthy and poor wage earners move between different households, and form important and lasting ties with extended kin outside of their natal families. However, fosterage rates are considerably lower among emigrants from Sikaiana (about one-half of the rate on Sikaiana). This difference suggests that fosterage is losing popularity among emigrants, and Sikaiana families are becoming more differentiated and isolated.

In the 20th century, new types of social relationships and interactional settings with new types of equalities and inequalities have been introduced into the Sikaiana social system. Nevertheless, thus far, Sikaiana remains a cohesive community with contexts for equality in institutionalized patterns of alcohol consumption, fosterage, interpersonal etiquette, and community participation in decision making. However, it is not yet clear whether newly introduced institutions eventually will alter indigenous social relationships, causing cleavages within, and defections from, the local community as its people become incorporated into a national polity.

Conclusion

A consideration of the nature of equality should include and examine the cultural definitions of the individual or the self and the expectations for behavior in various role relationships, interactional settings, and institutions. I have outlined the manner in which Sikaiana is an egalitarian society, although there are other contexts and institutions where relationships are unequal. It is possible to maintain inequality and equality in different ways within the same social system. Furthermore, different social systems use a variety of cultural ideologies to support relationships that are described as egalitarian (see Flanagan 1983 and his discussion of the *andau* relationship in this volume).

Rayner (this volume) suggests a basic distinction between systems that emphasize equality of opportunity as opposed to those that emphasize equality of outcomes. For example, leadership in many Melanesian political systems is sometimes described as egalitarian in terms of opportunities, although leaders emerge as a result of competition (see Sahlins 1963, Chowning 1973:22-25).[10] In contrast, Sikaiana expectations for humility, and institutions such as drinking groups, fosterage, and community participation in decision making emphasize equality of condition or outcomes.

Newly introduced social relationships on Sikaiana, however, entail new kinds of equalities and inequalities, both among the Sikaiana themselves and between the Sikaiana and other Solomon Islanders. Some Sikaiana social relationships are oriented to the indigenous community; others are oriented to participation in an outside, diverse, multi-ethnic, and differentiated social system. This examination of Sikaiana social relationships shows that it is possible to maintain certain types of egalitarian relationships in subsystems such as communities, and perhaps other social groupings (voluntary associations or clubs), that are different from those found in the larger, encompassing, social systems. Indeed, subsystems that are based upon egalitarian relationships may be valued by people who simultaneously participate in larger social systems that are based upon hierarchical and stratified social interactions. After 50 years of participation in new identities and relationships that are part of a regional and international social system often involving hierarchical and differentiated relationships, most Sikaiana continue to maintain a commitment to their indigenous community with its expectations and contexts for egalitarian relationships.

Notes

[1] This perspective is shaped by various writings on role theory including Linton 1936, Merton 1957, Parsons 1951, Parsons and Shils 1951, Goffman 1961, Goodenough 1965, Keesing 1970, Davenport 1976. I am indebted to discussions with Drs. William Davenport, Erving Goffman, Jane Goodale, and Ward Goodenough, all members of my dissertation committee at the University of Pennsylvania, for refining my thinking on these issues. They are, of course, in no way accountable for errors, nor do they necessarily agree with the perspective taken here. I also have incorporated helpful suggestions by this volume's editors.

[2] I did fieldwork on Sikaiana from October 1980 to July 1983 with funding from the National Science Foundation. Many of the issues discussed in this paper are discussed in more detail in Donner 1985.

[3] Some caveats are necessary. Most of the following discussion is focused on relationships between males. Women do not enjoy the same rights as men in terms of their access to land, and do not participate as fully in the atoll's political offices. Generally, however, women are committed to the institutions and values to be discussed. Relationships between men and women are complex, and would require an extended discussion beyond the scope of this paper (again see Donner 1985.) Moreover, I will examine Sikaiana interactions with one another; I will not discuss how the Sikaiana people interact with other Polynesian and Melanesian ethnic groups in the Solomon Islands.

[4] Not everyone subscribes to this version of land acquisition, although most people accept the de facto independence of these land-owning lineages. A fuller discussion of the subtleties of Sikaiana land tenure issues, and how these support egalitarian values, is found in Donner 1985.

[5] See for example Tikopia (Firth 1957).

[6] See examples from Tokelau (Huntsman 1971) and Tuvalu (Ellice Islands) (Noricks 1981); also general discussions by Goodenough 1955, Firth 1957.

[7] In another paper (Donner ms) being prepared for publication, I have described drinking behavior in greater detail, showing how the social organization of drinking reflects important egalitarian values. Again, some caveats are necessary. At times, men are competitive about the amount of toddy they are able to drink. Sometimes, drunken men do not follow Sikaiana values for modesty, and boast about their abilities. Alcohol consumption is an egalitarian activity in other societies (see Netting 1979:353, Robbins 1979:173).

[8] This kind of participation in community activities and social groups also is found in other neighboring, small-scale Polynesian societies such as Nukuoro (Carroll 1966) and Tokelau (Huntsman 1971); see also Simmel (1908/1971) for a general discussion of related issues.

[9] Sikaiana's decentralized leadership system is partly grounded in a lineage's independent rights to land. In contrast with Sikaiana, Luaniua, another Polynesian community with historical and cultural relationships with Sikaiana, seems to have been consolidating political power during the 19th century in a single leader or 'king,' the heku'u (see Hogbin 1931, Hogbin 1934:224-229, Sarfert and Damm 1929-31:310).

[10] Note that the type of egalitarian relationship between andau, described by Flanagan in this volume, is very different from those associated with big-man leadership.

Bibliography

Beteille, Andre 1986. 'Individualism and Equality.' In *Current Anthropology* 27:121-134.

Carroll, Vern 1966. 'Nukuoro Kinship.' PhD thesis, University of Chicago. Ann Arbor, Michigan: University Microfilms.

Chowning, Ann 1973. 'An Introduction to the Peoples and Cultures of Melanesia.' In Addison-Wesley Module in Anthropology no. 38. Reading, Mass: Addison-Wesley.

Davenport, William 1976. 'Kinship and Sentiment in Santa Cruz Island Society.' Seminar paper, University of Pennsylvania.

Donner, William n.d. '"The World as the World is Not": Toddy Drinking on a Polynesian Outlier.' Paper read at Social Anthropology Seminar, University of Pennsylvania. In preparation for publication.

Donner, William 1985. 'Sikaiana Social Organization: Social Categories Relationships in a Contemporary Polynesian Society.' PhD thesis, Anthropology Department, University of Pennsylvania.

Firth, Raymond 1957. (Original 1936.) *We, the Tikopia: A Sociological Study of Kinship in Primitive Polynesia.* Boston: Beacon House.

Firth, Raymond 1957. 'A Note on Descent Groups in Polynesia.' In *Man* 57:4-8.

Flanagan, James G. 1983. 'Wovan Social Organization.' PhD thesis, University of Pennsylvania.

Goffman, Erving 1961. *Encounters: Two Studies in the Sociology of Interaction.* Indianapolis: Free Press.

Goodenough, Ward 1955. 'A Problem in Malayo-Polynesian Social Organization.' In *American Anthropologist* 57:71-83.

Goodenough, Ward 1965. 'Rethinking "Status" and "Role": Toward a General Model of the Cultural Organization of Social Relationships.' In *The Relevance of Models For Social Anthropology* (ed) Michael Banton. A.S.A. Monograph no.1. New York: Tavistock.

Hogbin, Ian 1931. 'The Social Organization of Ontong Java.' In *Oceania* I:339-423.

Hogbin, Ian 1934. *Law and Order in Polynesia: A Study of Primitive Legal Institutions.* New York: Harcourt, Brace & Company.

Huntsman, Judith 1971. 'Kin and Coconuts on a Polynesian Atoll: Socio-economic Organization of Nukunonu, Tokelau Islands.' PhD Thesis, Bryn Mawr College. Ann Arbor, Michigan: University Microfilms.

Keesing, Roger 1970. 'Toward a Model of Role Analysis.' In *A Handbook of Method in Cultural Anthropology* (eds) R. Naroll and R. Cohen. New York: Columbia University Press.

Linton, Ralph 1936. *The Study of Man.* New York: Appleton-Century.

Merton, Robert 1957. 'The Role-Set: Problems in Sociological Theory.' In *British Journal of Sociology* 8:106-120.

Netting, Robert McC. 1979. 'Beer as a Locus of Value Among the West African Kofyar.' In *Beliefs, Behaviors, & Alcoholic Beverages: A Cross-Cultural Survey* (ed) Mac Marshall. Ann Arbor: The University of Michigan Press.

Noricks, Jay 1981. 'Niuato Kinship and Social Organization.' PhD thesis, University of Pennsylvania.

Parsons, Talcott 1951. *The Social System.* Glencoe, Illinois: The Free Press.

Parsons, Talcott and Edward Shils 1951. *Toward a General Theory of Social Action.* Cambridge: Harvard University Press.

Robbins, Richard Howard 1979. 'Alcohol and the Identity Struggle: Some Effects of Economic Change on Interpersonal Relations.' In *Beliefs, Behaviors, & Alcoholic Beverages: A Cross-Cultural Survey* (ed) Mac Marshall. Ann Arbor: The University of Michigan Press.

Sahlins, Marshall 1958. *Social Stratification in Polynesia.* Seattle and London: University of Washington Press.

Sahlins, Marshall 1963. '"Poor Man, Rich Man, Big-man, Chief": Political Types in Melanesia and Polynesia.' *Comparative Studies in Society and History* 5:285-303.

Sarfert, Ernst and Hans Damm 1929-31. *Luangiua und Nukumanu, Ergebunsse der Sudsee Expedition.* Abt 2 Ethnographie B. Mikronesien. Volume 12.

Simmel, Georg 1950. *The Sociology of Georg Simmel.* Translated, edited, and with an introduction by Kurt Wolff. New York: The Free Press.

Simmel, Georg 1908/1971. 'Group Expansion and the Development of Individuality.' In *Georg Simmel On Individuality and Social Forms* (ed) Donald E. Levine. Chicago and London: University of Chicago Press.

8 The cultural construction of equality on the New Guinea Highlands' fringe

JAMES G. FLANAGAN

ABSTRACT

The establishment of identity relationships through shared experience provides a frequently used mechanism for the subversion of hierarchy implicit in sibling order, initiation grading, or inter-ethnic difference. Based on data collected in the New Guinea Highlands and on comparative data on the Pacific, the creation of such identity relationships and their utility in extending community boundaries are examined. Treating interpersonal equality as a structural element in small-scale societies permits a fine-grained analysis of egalitarianism as a sociocultural model, desired state, or achieved end, and extends the analysis of ideology and behavior.

Introduction

In *Etoro Social Structure* (1977), a book that attained the well-deserved status of an instant classic among New Guinea anthropologists, Raymond Kelly criticized anthropologists for abandoning the analysis of structure in New Guinea when simple, unidimensional structural models would not suffice.

The concept of loose structure, so prominent in the New Guinea Highlands' literature in the 1960's and 1970's (see, for example, DuToit 1962, Pouwer 1960 and 1966, Watson 1970), rather than addressing the complexities of Highlands' social organization, was simply a convenient way of avoiding the analytical issues. The essence of social structure, for Kelly, is the 'organization of contradictions' (1977:3). These contradictions, obscured at the surface level by the contextual segregation of rules systems, are available to analysis at the level of deep structure. Their analysis permits the location of deviance within structure and the reintegration of behavior and rule or structure and empirical events.

This paper, following Kelly's lead, analyzes the structure of interpersonal relations, particularly interpersonal equality. In essence, it is an attempt to take the notion of friendship, the epitome of anti-structure, and lodge it firmly within the concept of structure. To achieve this, it is necessary to place the taken-for-granted facts of friendship into the problematic domain of structured relationships. In spite of its anti-structural appearance, friendship is governed by aesthetic principles, rights, duties, and obligations to as great an extent as anthropology's epitome of structure, kinship. Friendship is governed by rules of choice and appropriateness, and those rules, however anti-structural their initial appearance, should be amenable to analysis.

Much of the debate that has gone on in both sociology and anthropology (e.g. Britan and Cohen, eds 1980, Cohen and Service, eds 1978) has been concerned with a macro-political focus, with the structure of equality and inequality as it exists at the institutional level. This focus has permitted a range of definitions of an egalitarian structure depending on whether one adopts intentions or ends as the fundamental criterion upon which to construct the system. Oppenheim (1968:102-103) distinguishes between 'equality of characteristics' and 'equality of treatment' as defining principles in approaches to egalitarianism. Equality of characteristics focuses attention on those social attributes with respect to which men are to be considered equal. Normative statements about equality invariably concern treatment, although they may contain references to characteristics. To claim, for example, that 'all men are equal' can only mean that the attributes with respect to which they are equal are singled out as more significant than the attributes with respect to which they are unequal.

Alternatively, one may view equality by contrasting equality of opportunity with equality of outcome. Equal opportunity strategies are, in a sense, unconcerned with outcomes. The structure of opportunities is defined as egalitarian, subsequent inequalities are the product of individual initiative, intelligence etc. Strategies focusing on equality of outcomes must, of necessity, abandon socially imposed criteria of equal opportunities to ensure socially desired ends. Utopian communes, for example, are concerned with outcomes and impose a structured equality (frequently measured in economic terms) on the members (Daner 1979).

In a similar vein, but moving to more frequently cited anthropological contexts, !Kung bushmen are 'egalitarian' in terms of the structure of opportunities and largely in terms of economic outcomes (Lee and Devore 1968, Leacock and Lee 1982). New Guinea Highlanders are egalitarian in terms of the structure of opportunities, though not necessarily in terms of outcomes (e.g. Strathern 1971, 1983). Rules of inheritance and succession and the lack of capital accumulation in these exchange-dominated economies of New Guinea guarantee a measure of equality of opportunity for all male participants. Subsequent manipulation and the rewards of individual initiative, however, introduce substantial inequality (measured both in terms of economics and power) within a particular individual's lifetime. Systems with hereditary chieftainship or kingship are inegalitarian in terms of both opportunities and outcomes.

Note here, I am 'characterizing' systems, an approach long accepted in anthropology, but one that I hope to show as inadequate to handle the complexities of hierarchy and equality.

We should note also that western treatments of inequality and equality have focused largely on economic dimensions. This is understandable in the context of sociocultural sciences striving for measurable variables. Relative economic status is easily scaled. Attempts to measure alternative dimensions of inequality are much less successful, although recent analytical developments in grid/group analysis (Douglas 1970, and Gross and Rayner 1985) are promising beginnings. Differential knowledge, access to the supernatural, or skill are not easily measured and are complicated by being manifest in a variety of domains. Faced with societies where economic differentiation was not manifest, such as gatherer-hunters and small scale horticulturalists, anthropologists treated these societies as egalitarian. This is not to deny the utility of economics as one dimension in measuring inequality. Rather, my argument demands that we expand the dimensions of inequality to encompass all aspects of scarce-resource competition.

The economic approach ignored the competition for status, prestige, and privilege that was an everyday aspect of gatherer-hunter and small-scale horticulturalist societies. In doing so, this approach also ignored the rules and regulations inherent in these societies and the strategies adopted by persons within these systems to limit inequality or to ensure interpersonal equality. Equality is not just a natural outcome of lack of opportunity to develop inequities. It is culturally constructed in the context of interpersonal relations.

A serious limitation should be recognized immediately. I am concerned primarily with the relationship between men and men, secondarily with the relationship between women and women, and not at all with the relationship between women and men. This final area, perhaps the most significant domain of enquiry in contemporary anthropology, presents special problems both in the field and in theory formulation, and must be treated elsewhere. In part, the problems of cross-sex relationships derive from the ubiquity of sex as a significant differentiating principle cross-culturally, and, in part, derive from the long-standing theoretical tradition that gives primacy to the consideration of male-male relationships in the political domain. Western anthropology has defined the field of politics in such a way as to exclude female influence from the political decision-making process. Fortes' (1958) distinction of the jural and domestic categories, for example, takes such an exclusion as basic to the analytic strategy. Any complete analysis of equality generation and maintenance will have to take account of this distinction and resolve the dichotomies that rest upon it. In the meantime, the present paper is offered as a special case within the more general field of interpersonal relations.

It is evident from the foregoing, that anthropological approaches to the study of inequality in tribal societies have focused largely on institutional arrangements above or beyond the domain of kinship. Recently, however, a number of theorists have turned their attention to the inherent inequalities within kinship structures themselves (Keesing 1972). The position is well summarized by Beteille (1977:159) when he states that 'It is facile to oppose the principle of kinship to that of hierarchy for there are societies in which inequalities are articulated mainly through the system of kinship.' Indeed, as Beteille so aptly observes, kinship may not be merely a mode for the expression of inequality but may, in some cases, be the primary mode through which interpersonal inequality is expressed. By ignoring interpersonal inequality as expressed in intergenerational relationships, in male-female relationships, and in sibling birth order, we have artificially constructed egalitarian social organizations. As a result, we have failed to understand the nature of interpersonal relations in these societies, and we have floundered in our attempts to understand their kinship structures. As Keesing (1972:17) has commented, 'by taking kinship as our dominant model of tribal social order, we have become skilled decontextualizers... by focusing on kinship we have not learned how to make anthropological sense of friendship.'

The New Guinea Highlands' fringe

My own concerns with the nature of egalitarian relationships stem initially from a problem in Wovan kinship terminology. While observing the interaction of three young men who had undergone their adolescent initiation rites together, I noticed that individual A consistently used the term *andau* in address and reference to individual B, while always employing the term *noleva* in both addressing and referring to individual C. Individual B, for his part, also consistently used the term *noleva* in address and reference to individual C, but sometimes would initiate interactions with individual A or refer to him as *haul*. Individual C used *noleva* exclusively in both address and reference to both A and B. (See Figure 8.1).

Some basic knowledge of the Wovan and their kinship terminology is necessary to appreciate this complex interaction. The Wovan are a distinct cultural and linguistic group of some 700 swidden horticulturalists and pig herders who occupy the northern fringe of the Central Highlands of Papua New Guinea (Flanagan 1983). They are monogamous, practice virilocal residence in which, ideally, a set of male siblings establishes a single 'big house' together and resides there with its members' wives, unmarried children of both sexes, and married sons with their wives. They employ a patrilineal idiom in speaking of their descent groups despite a stated rule of parallel cousin marriage that frequently results in the marriage of close patrilateral kin. Wovan male youths pass

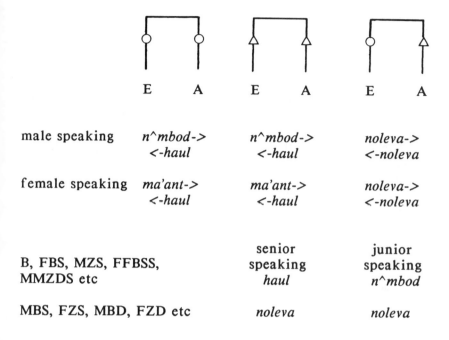

	E	A	E	A	E	A
male speaking	*n^mbod->* *<-haul*		*n^mbod->* *<-haul*		*noleva->* *<-noleva*	
female speaking	*ma'ant->* *<-haul*		*ma'ant->* *<-haul*		*noleva->* *<-noleva*	

	senior speaking *haul*	junior speaking *n^mbod*
B, FBS, MZS, FFBSS, MMZDS etc		
MBS, FZS, MBD, FZD etc	*noleva*	*noleva*

Figure 8.1: Same generation reciprocal kinship terms

As the Wovan use a variant of an Iroquois terminology, terminological distinctions are based on the relative sex of the connecting links in the generation immediately senior to ego (the parental generation). Thus, parallel or same-sex links yield a 'sibling' term, cross or opposite-sex links yield a 'cousin' term.

through an elaborate series of initiation rites that creates lasting bonds among the initiates and between initiates and their ritual sponsors. No such rites are held for females.

Like many highland peoples of Papua New Guinea, the Wovan employ a variant of an Iroquois kinship terminology. Siblings and parallel cousins are differentiated from cross cousins. While siblings are differentiated by both sex and seniority, cross cousins are grouped under a single term, *noleva*, that overrides both sex and seniority. Cross-sex siblings are assigned a single term (*marau*, male speaking, and *nolau*, female speaking) without respect to birth order or seniority. Same-sex siblings, however, are differentiated on the basis of seniority. Thus, for a male ego, the term *n^mbod* denotes an elder or senior same-sex sibling. This term is reciprocated by the term *haul*, younger or junior same-sex sibling. The respective terms for a female ego are *ma'ant* and *haul*. (The overriding of sex as a significant feature of juniors is common in PNG and extends throughout the Wovan kinship terminological system). (See Figure 8.2).

Thus, the three young men who sparked this initial interest are related to one another as follows:

A is a junior sibling of B
B is a senior sibling of A
A and B are cross cousins of C

When abiding by strict kinship terminological usage, A should call B *n^mbod*, B should call A *haul*, A and B should call C by the self-reciprocal term *noleva*. We find the third of these possibilities being employed consistently, the second being employed sporadically, and the first being consistently overridden in favor of the term *andau*.

Elsewhere, I have treated the self-reciprocal Wovan term *andau* in detail. I glossed the term 'partnership' (Flanagan unpublished manuscript 1982), and defined it as denoting any two persons who are perceived, and perceive themselves, to be equivalent with respect to a third outside object or event. Technically, if A:X :: B:X, then, A and B are *andau* to one another. The term is used by, among other pairs, men who have served on coastal plantations together, men who are trading partners to one another, men who have undergone initiation together, women who have married into the same house, persons (either two males or two females) who share the same name. Even a cursory inspection of this list of usages draws our attention to two significant features; the

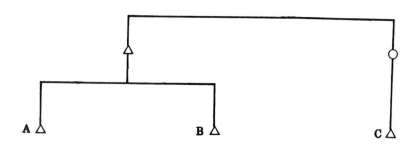

A > B	*haul* or *andau*	Reciprocal B > A	*andau*
A > C	*noleva*	C > A	*noleva*
B > C	*noleva*	C > B	*noleva*

Figure 8.2   Terms of Address and Reference

reciprocal users of the term always have shared a significant experience or relationship to a series of events or objects. In all cases the pairs using the term *andau* are of the same sex.

What is actually occurring in the interaction described above? This, I should add, was not an idiosyncratic piece of interaction, but was supported by a number of other observations made later. All three youths were co-initiates and thus entitled to use the term *andau* with each other. None chose to use the term in preference to the kinship term *noleva* (cross cousin) where this could be legitimately used. The younger sibling consistently used the term in preference to *n^mbod* while the elder sibling showed some variability.

The Wovan, too, obviously are operating on criteria of equality of characteristics. The sharing of certain traits or experiences is used to 'define' those individuals who share them as equal in some significant sense. They are not, however, content to limit the definition of equality to a strict economic dimension. In a society where economic differentiation is minimal, alternative dimensions of inequality are emphasized.

The lack of polarity in the *noleva* term is the key to its continued use. The polarity of the *n^mbod-haul* set is a recognition of seniority and authority built into the terminology. The younger (junior) sibling, in this case, is using the shared experience of co-initiation to forge an egalitarian relationship with his senior sibling, and is marking that relationship by the use of the term *andau*. The senior sibling largely accepts this equality while occasionally reverting to the pre-initiated hierarchical ordering of siblingship.

In this instance, the fortuitous juxtaposition of a set of kinship terms with a term outside the domain of kinship provides insight both to the nature of Wovan social relationships and the structure of Wovan kinship. The hierarchical ordering of siblings is manifest in the terminology and the overriding of sex distinctions among juniors (this pattern is repeated in the grandparent-grandchild set of terms). The same-sex specificity of the term *andau* also draws our attention to the fundamental position that sex distinctions occupy in Wovan construction of social relationships and in Wovan identity concepts.

More significantly, however, this interaction draws our attention to the social creation of equality and the necessity of its reaffirmation and maintenance. Sharing of experiences has been widely documented as a basis upon which egalitarian relationships are formed, but as anthropologists, we have spent very little time analyzing the interactional strategies pursued in maintaining that equality. By focusing attention on the strategies by which humans manage to create inequality, we have neglected its counterpart; the strategies by which humans create and maintain equality.

In Wovan idiom, all men are big once they have passed through the full initiation sequence, but this does not guarantee their fundamental equality. Equality is generated in the initiation sequence, in the performance of coastal plantation service, and in the subsequent performance of the duties of an equal. As kinship devolves from fulfillment of kinship duties, equality devolves from action. Trade partners, for example, are equal in the context of their trading relationship. But trade partners of Wovan men are frequently drawn from different ethnic groups; therefore, by entering into a trade partnership, participants undertake obligations far beyond the trading relationship itself. They guarantee the security and well-being of their partner as well as honesty in dealing with him. To cheat a partner or to renege upon him is equivalent to cheating oneself, and is a denial of the fundamental basis of the entire relationship.

Some comparative cases

The Wovan case described here is not unusual in the ethnography of Papua New Guinea, although I would argue that notions of 'brotherhood,' 'siblingship,' or 'fictive kinship' that have frequently been applied to these relationships tend to mask their cultural aim and their dynamic and achieved status.

Lindenbaum and Glasse (1969) provide evidence of the existence of 'age-mate' equality among the Fore of the Eastern Highlands of Papua New Guinea. They note that the relationship *nagaiye*, glossed as age mate, 'denotes a relationship of equivalence and solidarity' (1969:165). South Fore men 'rarely list their immediate kin as age mates' (1969:168). Lindenbaum and Glasse interpret this fact as being indicative of the emphasis on lineage ties over coeval bonds. However, they go on to state, 'age mates address and refer to each other as *nagaiye* in contexts where kin terms would otherwise be employed' (1969:168). *Nagaiye* are said to regard each other as 'twin brothers or symbolic equivalents of themselves' (1969:172).

More recently, Shirley Lindenbaum (1979) has outlined a variety of relationships among the Fore that corresponds closely to those I have labeled partnership. She particularly notes the trading partnership as a relationship that extends community boundaries by the use of an egalitarian idiom.

Leroy (1981) has presented an extensive case for the equivalence of sibling pairs in Kewa narratives. Kewa Ancestries are presented using formulaic pairings of male siblings begetting similarly formulaic pairs of male offspring. Although I would argue for the fundamental inequality of siblings, we may have a case here for structural manipulation in narrative. The Kewa, it would appear, are as prone as anthropologists to perceive genealogically or temporally remote siblings as equivalent. Significantly, however, in formal genealogical elicitation settings, Leroy never encountered this narrative formula.

The cases presented so far are only a sample of the reported equivalency relationships on mainland New Guinea. These cases are sufficient to demonstrate that we are not dealing with a phenomenon of limited distribution, nor are such equivalency relationships confined to mainland New Guinea. Chowning and Goodenough (1971) have drawn attention to 'formalized' relationships that exist between persons who are not consanguineal kin among the Lakalai of New Britain. One such equivalency pair discussed by Chowning and Goodenough consists of men who 'are paired together in the dance at a memorial feast for the dead.' Burridge (1957, 1959) drew attention to the possibility of constructing egalitarian relationships between non-kin on the basis of kinship extension or metaphorical kinship. The *kwav* relationship, which he glosses as 'friend,' is a 'one to one relationship between two individuals, between men or between women, but never between a man and a woman' (Burridge 1957:178). Firth (1936), in describing the *tau soa* relationship in Tikopia, glossed it as bond friendship emphasizing a 'life-long bond, reinforced and expressed by reciprocal obligations, mutual trust and periodical exchange of gifts' (1936:259). Recently, in an insightful paper on the Buid of Mindoro, Gibson (1985) has contrasted 'companionship' and 'kinship' on precisely the same dimensions I have employed here. Companionship, based on shared activity, is presented as a relationship of equality.

Throughout the Pacific, we find institutionalized mechanisms and interpersonal strategies to promote egalitarian social relationships in the face of socially maintained and biologically imposed inequalities. The egalitarian relationships thereby created are not merely a natural outcome of insufficient resources, nor are these relationships, once achieved, so stable as to require no further manipulation. Kinship theorists, studying the phenomena of genealogical manipulation and the creation of fictive kin, have long appreciated that persons regard each other as kin because they behave toward one another as kin. Similarly, it would appear that persons regard each other as equal because they behave toward one another as equals. Such equality requires regular reaffirmation on the part of both members of the dyadic relationship.

The recent literature on age grading (especially in East Africa) is also useful in elucidating the Wovan material. LaFontaine (1978:13) states that 'the elementary structure of age-differentiation is the articulation of relations of inequality and equality.' Age grading, according to Baxter and Almagor (1978:159), is probably universal and places a social stamp on the biological process of aging. As they so nicely put it, 'age systems are a device to make the cruel descent through life to decay appear as if it were an ascent to a superior, because senior, condition' (1978: 176). Age grading serves to establish a hierarchical order by emphasizing the similarities of those within age grades while emphasizing the differences between those in different age grades. 'The common fact of all such differentiating systems is that the boundaries are marked by ritual and that the classes thus constituted are associated with contrasted sets of behavior and moral qualities' (LaFontaine 1978:13).

Wovan initiation places the initiate in a position on a hierarchical structure that is entered through initiation and is defined by the number of initiations one has undergone. It places the youth, in Spencer's phrase, on the 'gerontocratic ladder' (1976). Thus, as East African theorists have long appreciated, the society is defined in terms of a hierarchical order.

However, this example draws attention to the element of time in any analysis of hierarchy, since over the course of an individual's life, he may participate in all levels of the hierarchical structure. A straightforward equal-opportunities approach to hierarchy and equality leads to the conclusion that these societies are egalitarian. There are no valued statuses in the institutional structure from which particular persons are excluded. Therefore, at the interpersonal rather

175

than institutional level, we must be aware of the gerontocratic hierarchy and the strategies people employ to achieve and maintain interpersonal equality.

Conclusion

In the past, the lack of institutionalized political leadership roles has led us to classify New Guinea Highlands' societies as 'egalitarian.' All men may, at least in theory, compete for big man status. Studies of the inegalitarian aspects of these societies have dealt mainly with male-female relations (e.g. Brown and Buchbinder 1976). The Wovan material, I believe, draws our attention to the construction and maintenance of equality. Egalitarian relationships, established by ritual or other behavioral means, are not, as Glasse and Lindenbaum have suggested for the Fore, 'relationships of playfulness and freedom standing outside the power structure' (1969:172), but rather, are integral to that power structure. The nature of the partner relationship permits the establishment of relationships of friendship and equality that transcend, not only the domain of kinship, but even ethnic boundaries, and thereby, provide a basis for the conduct of interpersonal relations.

In this paper, I have focused attention on the rules that operate to maintain interpersonal equality in the face of socially institutionalized hierarchy and natural biological inequalities. We cannot expect such rules to be simple or immediately apparent. As Edgerton (1985:206) has observed, 'because social living anywhere is, to say the least, always complex, specific rules, too, like meta-rules, may overlap or conflict. As a result, some rules may be construed as hierarchical, with one being more important than another, or they may be seen as context-specific.' The context specificity of rules that permits contextual segregation of rule systems also permits the coexistence of hierarchical and egalitarian structures.

An enquiry into the nature of equality within social systems is, of necessity, an enquiry into the culturally salient characteristics with respect to which persons in those systems are regarded as equal. It takes us beyond the concept itself into those features of personhood that are fundamental aspects of the cultural system. This view suggests that, whatever its attractiveness as a shorthand/indexical expression, the idea of egalitarian and inegalitarian societies may mask the very problem into which we wish to enquire. Anthropology long has abandoned such expressions as 'the X are a patrilineal society' in favor of detailed analyses of groups in such societies that employ a patrilineal idiom in recruitment of members, or the contexts in which such idioms are employed. Following the lead of the kinship theorists, we also should abandon such expressions as 'the Y are an egalitarian society' in favor of analyses of the groups or dyads that employ an egalitarian idiom, the contexts in which the idiom is employed, and the relationship of that idiom to the total cultural order. Such analyses would have to take special notice of the interactional and behavioral strategies employed by members of the society and of the variety of valued or scarce resources including knowledge, power, and material possessions available for manipulation. Such analyses not only will encourage the refinement of the concepts of hierarchy and equality, but also will reap benefits in a more adequate understanding of the nature of social order in both tribal and non-tribal societies.

Bibliography

Baxter, P., and U. Almagor (eds) 1978. *Age, Generation and Time*. New York: St. Martins Press.

Beteille, Andre 1977. *Inequality Among Men*. Oxford: Basil Blackwell.

Britan, Gerald M. and Ronald Cohen (eds) 1980. *Hierarchy and Society*. Philadelphia: ISHI.

Brown, Paula, and Georgeda Buchbinder (eds) 1976. *Man and Woman in the New Guinea Highlands*. Washington: American Anthropological Association Special Publication No. 8.

Burridge, Kenhelm 1957. 'Friendship in Tangu.' In *Oceania* 27:177-189.

Burridge, Kenhelm 1959. 'Siblingship in Tangu.' In *Oceania* 30:128-154.

Chowning, A., and W.H. Goodenough 1971. 'Lakalai Political Organization.' In *Politics in New Guinea* (eds) Ronald Berndt and Peter Lawrence. Nedlands: University of Western Australia Press.

Cohen, Ronald and Elman R. Service 1978. *Origins of the State*. Philadelphia: ISHI.

Daner, E. 1979. *The American Children of Krsna*. New York: Holt, Rinehart and Winston.

Douglas, Mary 1970. *Natural Symbols*. London: Barrie and Rockliffe.

DuToit, Brian M. 1962. 'Structural Looseness in New Guinea.' *Journal of the Polynesian Society* 71:397-399.

Edgerton, Robert B. 1985. *Rules, Exceptions and Social Order*. Berkeley: University of California Press.

Firth, Raymond 1936. 'Bond Friendship in Tikopia.' In *Custom is King* (ed) L.H.D. Buxton. London: Hutchinson.

Flanagan, James G. n.d. 'Siblingship and Partnership.' Manuscript on file.

Flanagan, James G. 1983. 'Wovan Social Organization.' PhD thesis, University of Pennsylvania.

Fortes, Meyer 1958. 'Introduction.' In *The Developmental Cycle in Domestic Groups* (ed) Jack Goody. Cambridge: Cambridge University Press.

Gibson, Thomas 1985. 'The Sharing of Substance Versus the Sharing of Activity Among the Buid.' In *Man* 20:391-411.

Glasse, R. and S. Lindenbaum 1980. 'South Fore Kinship.' In *Blood and Semen* (eds) E. Cook and D. O'Brien. Ann Arbor: University of Michigan Press.

Gross, Jonathan and Steve Rayner 1985. *Measuring Culture.* New York: Columbia University Press.

Keesing, Roger 1972. 'Simple Models of Complexity: The Lure of Kinship.' In *Kinship Studies in the Morgan Centennial Year* (ed) P. Reining. Washington: Anthropological Society of Washington.

Kelly, Raymond 1977. *Etoro Social Structure.* Ann Arbor: University of Michigan Press.

LaFontaine, J. 1978. *Sex and Age as Principles of Social Differentiation.* London: Academic Press.

Leacock, Eleanor and Richard Lee (eds) 1982. *Politics and History in Band Societies.* Cambridge: Cambridge University Press.

Lee, Richard and Irven DeVore (eds) 1968. *Man the Hunter.* Chicago: Aldine.

Leroy, J. 1981. 'Siblingship and Descent in Kewa Ancestries.' *American Anthropologist* 83:900-905.

Lindenbaum, S. 1979. *Kuru Sorcery*. Palo Alto: Mayfield.

Lindenbaum, S. and R. Glasse 1969. 'Fore Age Mates.' In *Oceania* 39:165-173

Oppenheim, F. 1968. 'The Concept of Equality.' In *International Encyclopedia of the Social Sciences* (ed) D. Sills. New York: Free Press.

Pouwer, Jan 1960. 'Loosely Structured Societies in Netherlands New Guinea.' In *Bijdragen tot de Taal-Land-en Volkenkunde* 116:109-118.

Pouwer, Jan 1966. 'Structure and Flexibility in a New Guinea Society.' *Bijdragen tot de Taal-Land-en Volkenkunde.* 122:158-169.

Spencer, Paul 1976. 'Opposing Streams and the Gerontocratic Ladder: Two Models of Age Organization in East Africa.' In *Man* 11:153-175.

Strathern, Andrew 1971. *The Rope of Moka*. Cambridge: Cambridge University Press.

Strathern, Andrew (ed) 1983. *Inequalities in New Guinea Highlands Societies.* Cambridge: Cambridge University Press.

Watson, James B. 1970. 'Society as Organized Flow: The Tairora Case.' *South Western Journal of Anthropology* 26:107-124.

Index

egalitarianism (cont.)
individual vs collective
14, 15, 32, 115, 118-
120, 132-137, 139
meanings of 64
rise of in Digo society
117-118
vs hierarchy 56-58, 119-
120, 137-139
Ehrlich, E. 81, 95
Elite, see Kibbutzim
Engels, Frederick 5, 7, 17
Entryism 30
Equality
access to services 45-
46, 48, 63
anthropological study of
1-3
coexistence with
inequality 13, 14,
16, 157
concept of 9-11
definitions of 2, 157,
165, 176-177
economic dimensions of
166-167
equity, see Equality of
opportunity
equity vs strict equality
22, 30-31
historical primacy of 2
individual 31-37, 146-
153, 165, 168-176
interpersonal 11-12, 16,
146, 148-155, 164-
165, 167-176
maintenance of 2-3, 15,
103, 167, 172-173,
175
moral 13, 14, 16, 21, 103
of condition (strict
equality) 13, 14, 16,
20-22, 32, 61, 64-65,
157, 166

of opportunity (equity)
13, 14, 22, 30-31,
64-65, 166
origin and variety of 2
primitive 5-8
state of Grace vs state
of nature 3, 4, 12
structure of 165
vs inequality 1-8
Etoro Social Structure 164
Evans-Pritchard, E.E. 8, 9,
10, 18, 114, 117,
141, 142
Evolution
biological 7
of sociocultural forms
1, 5-8, 10, 13
political 10
theorists of cultural 4,
7
Expulsion 23, 24, 27, 86
Factions, see Leadership
FAGOR 43, 44, 48, 67
Fairness criteria 40
Firth, Raymond 159-161,
174, 179
Fissioning, see Schism
Fitzpatrick, P. 90, 91, 95
Flanagan, James G. 157,
160, 161, 168, 170,
179
Forde, C.D. 115, 141
Fore 173-174
Fortes, M. 8, 9, 10, 18,
114, 117, 142, 167,
179
Fosterage 151-152, 156
Fourth International 23
Free riders, see
Cooperatives,
deviance 15, 21,
71, 80
Fried, Morton 9, 18